Content

Vol 93 No 4 Winter 2003/4

Poems

Essays

Reviews

Poet in the Gallery

Art

Poems

Daljit Nagra

LOOK WE HAVE COMING TO DOVER!

So various, so beautiful, so new – Matthew Arnold, "Dover Beach"

Stowed in the sea to invade
the lash alfresco of a diesel-breeze
ratcheting speed into the tide with brunt
gobfuls of surf phlegmed by cushy,
come-and-go tourists prow'd on the cruisers, lording the waves.

Seagull and shoal life bletching
vexed blarnies at our camouflage past
the vast crumble of scummed cliffs.
Thunder in its bluster unbladdering yobbish
rain and wind on our escape, hutched in a Bedford van.

Seasons or years we reap
inland, unclocked by the national eye
or a stab in the back, teemed for breathing
sweeps of grass through the whistling asthma
of parks, burdened, hushed, poling sparks across pylon and pylon.

Swarms of us, grafting
in the black within shot of the moon's spotlight,
banking on the miracle of sun to span
its rainbow, passport us to life. Only then
can it be human to bare-faced, hoick ourselves for the clear.

Imagine my love and I,
and our sundry others, blared in the cash
of our beeswax'd cars, our crash clothes,
free, as we sip from an unparasol'd table
babbling our lingoes, flecked by the chalk of Britannia.

John Haynes

from LETTER TO PATIENCE

XLIX

Outside, the almost coming first light shows
things as the shadows of themselves before
colour, thickness and English names enclose

their shapeless ghosts inside their shapes once more.
No word for it, except the glossary
of Sweet's Old English Reader, has this word-store

word for what seems now a more third worldly
kind of time, the-hour-before-dawn: *uhta.*
That guy a thousand years ago, maybe,

gone schizoid with remorse, or just a hearer
of voices, was voices, still is, still rows
across his moody ocean. *Anhaga,*

somebody who's hedged in, who also knows
how not being dead when others are, is to:
"experience the curving sky one goes

towards as one's own curving skull." "Untrue!
Untrue!" they shout, "No belly-aching yet
ever changed any coward's Fate." On cue

they float in rippling mail on the sea fret
towards him as he's screaming their names straight
into their faces, as he blubbers: "Let

me just explain!" and they disintegrate
into the almost coming dawn. A con.
A sentence from Boethius on Fate.

"And you dream. That the Führer's hand rests on
your hair again. You're his, you're his, you swear.
Then wake remembering high stone walls gone

to ruin, the work of giants, standing there
abandoned completely. You watch the breeze
blow dust like your own breath into that air.

Here Fate finished them off as if to please
the need for closure in a narrative
and leave nothing." Except some elegy's

hit and miss flights from lip and to lip, some native
pagan lay altered to make it flow
out of the quill of some monk trying to give

some soul a Christian course he couldn't know
was there. Download it. There's the parchment, stains
and all. *Anhaga: hedged around*, and so

enclosed – caught in the bone cell of the brains.
An which is one, and *haga*: hedge, akin
to hawthorn, hodge, Hodges, Hay, Hayward, Haynes,

that ghost in the machine nobody's in,
that Haynes the Englishman, his aspirate,
his diphthong, his nasal, his final thin

voiced sibilant, his lips and tongue estate,
his squirl of ink, one with the Windies bat
and Fulham wizard, thorn and leaf, the great

house built of sugar, and slavery. *That,
this, here, there, I, you*. Abi, yu deh grin,
Patience. Your feet even in heels are flat.

HARMONIES

in memory of my father

Margate, Westbrook Pavilion.
Twelve years old, I sit
at the dim-silver piano

in the orchestra pit.
Your then stronger arms are reaching
round the shoulders of my T-shirt.

Chord by chord you're teaching me:
The Man I Love,
those stepping-down harmonies –

which I can still just
remember if I
leave it to the finger muscles,

close my eyes,
and try not to try.

John Kinsella

POLLEN

As dust to the cuffs of trousers,
puff, atomise; black-cored planets
launching yellow satellites,
as trailing through uninhabited pasture:
wild oats, daisies, salvation jane, lupin flowers.
This body, a carry-all, a vehicle for reform;
anarchic pollination in the hungry appetite
of trails heading out from home;
this annual inculcation, infusing
histamine, voltage that alters
the structure of cells . . .
and so I leave again
and wash away the quarantine
the segregation
these writers of history who'd have all settlers
feel comfortable with pollen on the cuffs of trousers, identikit
as red around the eyes, these inflammations, these referendums –
furiously bright in the spring sunshine,
striking up discussions, confident as bees
almost stalling, but breaking
away – laden – just in time,
our instinctive, driven
representatives.

GRAPHOLOGY 43: PRE-CODE

These set-piece stanzas
override occult woman
with a grip on: they kissed
and still all vivisected:
lyrically, an ear of wheat
shed as they kissed,
and the species
consolidated. I can smile,
I can smile if I try.
A bower bird,
I lift the rusty gadget
and make hay, clarify.
It's light. Merrill Lynch
knows why, as talent
hangdogs, searchlights.
Moon over, hung over
moon as giddy
as a skylight.
Pavilion,
there on the green
spreadsheet: skittish
bendback,
skirting the room
as if no tree
ever made it.
Stuck across:
bridge, fence,
spotlight.

GRAPHOLOGY 60

Detunes and trauma counsellings
tender tawny frogmouths and spittoons,
        the dash across sand on Port Beach,
prior the flat-top, reactor off-shore,
        a rub down in winter sand. So, I prevaricate
and testiculate, those swallows cutting over the froth,
        small waves in toss and tow,
costs a lot to reclaim your goods from off-the-ship,
        trucks roaring through Rous Head,
docks and gantries, containers coming in
        for quarantine: a customs book
is the record of everything ever made,
        its true contents. There's such a thing
as hippopotamus oil. All terror's in there,
        like writing a verse novel
based on Bram Stoker's *inner*-Dracula,
        inner in its setting and character,
all commissar and commiserate at Cosi, the stressed poly,
        the God-need and wanting out
of quarrelling. And so it goes. Such is life.
        An itinerary. Safe travelling.
        Blood-on-the-dance-floor.

GRAPHOLOGY 61

Drove out into the official OUTBACK
and noted the cut-back
Mount Gibson, a back-
burner of a scrub nodule, to the back
of my memory and before Paynes Find, back-
tracked as never found, that hematite low-quality load; back
off! The 'roos in the roadtrains' beams, their backs
to the wall as bent to spring: back
then, they'd have bounded back
to where they'd come from without a crossing, backed
to the hilt by family, friends; goldminers; wary of the pastoralist back
at it with plough and crops so low a new type of machine is backed
by investors to lift the scanty grain back,
a lightning strike scorching through, ripping it back.

3.50 P.M., SUNDAY 21ST SEPT 2003

The window picture
slipped in the high winds,
lashing, swirling about
the swats of eucalypt leaves,
as if all that water
had weakened the frame,
and still one side of the tree
partially dry,
galahs sucking the weather up,
apt as moods,
transcendent shade
at the height of day.

Michael Henry

BITTEN BY THE MUSE

Hot nights swatting mosquitoes,
chasing the two-stroke hum of them.
In the morning red pointillist smudges
repousséed with limbs and thorax
like Japanese characters.
That *jaillissement* or spurt of blood
that Pierre Reverdy said was poetry.

We visit the Abbaye de Solesmes
near where the poet used to live.
Such a Leviticus of silence
that even my non-religious father
was impressed. What is the Trappist
for love? For service? For devotion?

We come out into the spoken world
and more mosquito bites. In the car
a sudden gushing forth of poetry,
kilometre after kilometre
it goes on. My mother in the front
shoots back an adulatory glance.

To think that I might have been bitten
by the same mosquito that bit
Pierre Reverdy when he was writing
the poems Frank O'Hara had
in his pocket when . . .

Lucie McKee

CURSE

The little immediate business of
adjusting to somebody's total
foreignness while at the same time
melting into the amniotic fluid
of love filling even my nostrils with
asphyxiating life and death and
resurrection so help me God and
damn the religious for so co-opting
the language of intensity I have no
other in my need but this totally
false pauper's tongue which I plead
guilty to in my crisis of want when
I'm not so quick as to go it alone
making it all up as I scrape along
is driving me so bananas that I yell
Go, Tigers, Go! Go straight to Hell.

GREEN BANANAS

Green bananas splayed out in a basket –
not a very elegant basket,
though it has a, more or less, graceful
handle (repaired with duct tape)
arced over a curved base. Still, it could be
a painting, duct tape and all, to show
how life really is, to show that green
bananas will lie down anywhere,
splayed out from a stem, broken
off from a huge bunch, chopped out
of a republic built on green
bananas. As I write, the fruit yellows
in the sour February light, and is entirely
the most beautiful thing I've seen
all day: green, with yellow wipes, black
nosed as a stuffed bear. Somewhere
there is sun enough to spring
these bananas to life, though they
were hacked down in their very prime
for me in my sunless, northern
kitchen. What other communion do
I need than with these gold-
turning green bananas, and with all
the hands and feet that laid them
in this basket. Here is our photograph.

Fiona Sampson

HOTEL CASINO

Everything writing itself into the
book the skin of page the white

what is *not known*
                              smudge
inky under eyes, under the reading line

a lash moving against cheek is a pointer
you could mouth it mouth the tenderness

chora
sweep up all the detail of your belly

black *barbe* black line of eye

the park with the babies, dogs.
                                        Pensioners.

                    *

Fairground browse and grab:
a park with tortoises. Kissing under trees.

Cartier Bresson's bodies are spilled on lawns
in Westpoint and Istanbul. Murmur of kissing

under the dark of Kalemegdan
vous les jeunes: in fifth-floor dark

the new red of the rail darkens and dries.

A packed dark in which the apartment
the pilot the student the mafioso
                                        music
falling like leaves.

*

Tired skin like paper the opposite of black
the tired yellow bear sleeps

in the big white bed

white sheets a knotted page, *signe*

de toi,
            signs of you in my body
on my skin,
                    smoked glass in the *ascenseur*

in the refracted street a kiosk
in the orchard a ladder
                            in the Metro

smart glossy all falls apart
mirrors of hair.

*

Disapproval like a gasp
flexes opens beyond this minute

the minute of presence before its
shuttered image
                    before the circling of mouths
kissing their zero sums
                            before subtraction.
Comfort me with apples
lips dosing on skin
juice springing across the tongue

obliteration of
obliteration.

*

Long regression of Germany
flatlands sunlight cows
                    the hand

moving away slowly the grasped hand
sliding on glass still
                    seen is a touch holding

up and there are strings between them
strings of atom sensation symbol flying

the length of a concrete platform

smear of country beyond closed window.

The star of broken glass.
Radiance of tape.

*

The book of remembering of forgetting
fear the wet white screen your eye mine

as if touching, dirt
scenting the skin, sweat a seal

asleep in a slick of hair grief cold
language lies around abandoned

and my
        and my
                night-time furniture useless heart
ticker-ticking yours

much that is forbidden touching cheek-bones gently
from the leaning walls.

Eva Salzman

INNU

It's a habit now, –
seven hours of blank staring
until the TV map jerks west enough
for landfall, the very first: Goose Bay. Goose Bay.

I'm hooked on the sound.
Can't you just see it, startled congregants
of the coast, ignited into a glorious fire, a storm
of feather and the deafening gripes of warning or distress?

Goose Bay:
for the connoisseur of desolate land,
the connoisseur of the word, emptied of all but tundra
and icy waste. Even their suicide rate soars romantically.

Who wishes to land
among the frozen garden dumps
to hear the parents say: *Take our children . . . Please.*
To meet these children grouped in the streets, laughing too loudly

and breathing, breathing
from the garbage bags of gas
clutched like wheezing babies to their chest,
like a host of Iron Lungs keeping alive the already dead.

Julian Stannard

BARBERA

I've got a bottle of *Barbera* but Lucia's out.
She must have a tire-bouchon, a something.

The bottle of *Barbera* is purple-red
and I've got some pasta on the go.
I *do* want to open that bottle of *Barbera*.

The Moroccans don't have a tire-bouchon.
The Chinese won't even open the door.
Should I try those people from Buenos Aires?

Dogs yap and spill onto the stairs.
An old woman stands on one side of the table.
Her son is holding open the door.

There's a bottle of *Barbera* on the table.
They smile when I explain why I'm there.
They ask me in for a glass of *Barbera*.

RIVIERA NIGHT TRAIN

The night train along the Riviera picked up pace:
windows open, we were airbrushed and buffeted.
I could smell sea-bream floating out there in the water.
I had to mark a hundred papers before we stepped down at *Principe*.
Sometimes the giddy scripts just leapt into the night.

Robert Hamberger

AFTER LORCA: *a version of* Sonnets of Dark Love

Sonnet of the garland of roses

I'm dying for that garland.
Weave it quickly, and while your fingers
work between petals and thorns
sing, groan, sing.
Its shadow disturbs my throat
a thousand times in this January light.

Between what you want of me and I of you
a breeze trembles the stars,
(is it stars or anemones?) rising.
This year has been one dark groan.

Eat the thicket of my wound,
lap what may be honey or blood from my thigh.

But quickly! The broken mouth of love,
that bitten soul, meet together in time and are destroyed.

Sonnet of the sweet complaint

I'm afraid of losing the wonder
of your eyes, or the lonely rose
of your breath stroking my cheek
through the night.

I'm dumped on this shore
like a trunk without branches,
my pain a squirming worm no sparrow
could notice, let alone eat.

If you're my buried treasure
my cross and my wet sorrow,
if I'm your lordship's dog

don't let me lose what I've found,
becoming the first leaf of autumn
drifting on your river, slipped away.

Wounds of love

This light, this swallowing fire.
These grey rocks blocking me in.
This hurt is my only idea:
the ache of heaven, the world, every hour.

Tears might slash my unstrung lyre:
these waves hitting me;
this scorpion stinging my breast.

These are love's burnt garlands:
this bed a battlefield
where I dream of your arms, your breath, your kisses
ruining my sleep.

Although I seek the height of good sense
give me your heart instead. Its cool valley
grows hemlock and a taste of bitter truth.

Sonnet of the letter

I wait for a word from you.
Nothing comes, and while that flower fades
I could give up myself, and you,
in the same suspended breath.

Air is immortal, stone inert,
neither wanting sun nor feeling it.
The heart dismisses cold honey
trickling down from the moon.

I suffered you. I strummed my fingers,
tiger and dove, across your waist
in our duel of bites and lilies.

Glut my madness with words
or leave me dipped in silence:
a dark night sailing a darker soul.

The poet speaks the truth

I want to tell you about my grief
so you'll weep for me, desire me
in a dusk of nightingales
with a dagger, with kisses, with you.

I want to kill the only witness
to the assassination of my flowers
and turn my sweat and crying
into a heap of ice or wheat.

Let's strum the strings
of I want you, you want me, always hunting
a milky sun, an ageing moon.

What you don't give and I won't ask for
will come through death, leaving
no shadow, no shiver of leaf on skin.

The poet speaks to his love on the telephone

Your voice washed my heart's sand-dune
in that cabin hidden by hills.
To the south of my feet it was spring,
to the north of my face a flower.

A pine-tree lit my narrow space
and sang without dawn, without a river.
For the first time my grief looped
crowns of hope around the roof.

Your far voice blossomed in me:
your honeycomb words,
your mouth feeding my ear.

Distant as an injured doe,
sweet as a sob through snowfall:
such sweet distance buzzing in my veins.

The poet asks his love about the 'enchanted city' of Cuenca

Did you like that city carved from water
drop by drop among pine-trees?
Did you notice dreams in the kerbs
and walls of pain blurred between cloud?

Did you catch the moon's icicle
melted by Jucar's crystal song?
Did hawthorn kiss your fingers,
crowning the distance with love?

Did you remember me when you rose
through silence, which the snake endures:
a prisoner of crickets and shadows?

Didn't you sense through empty air
a dahlia of agony and joy
spun at you from my heart's fire?

Gongoran sonnet in which the poet sends a pigeon to his love

This Turian dove is a gift.
Its white feathers
spill and bristle slow tongues of love
flickering on Greek laurel.

Its innocent strength, its soft neck
become linen of wind-whipped spray,
frost of dropped pearls, a smoky mist
singing your mouth's absence.

Stroke your hand across its colour
and you'll feel snowy music
blossom in flakes over your face.

Thus my heart at midnight and noon
caught in its cage of dark love
weeps when I can't fly to you.

Secret voice of dark love

Oh secret voice of dark love!
This shaven bleat, this injury,
bitter water, a sunk camelia.
Walls drop from the city, tides flinch from the sea.

This night I shout through:
my narrow distress a wet alley
where a dog gnaws the heart's gristle
and a lily dries like a throat.

Shun me, hot voice of ice.
Lose me at last among nettles
where my skin catches alight.

Empty my ivory head: this echoing bone.
Snap my pain in half
because I sing like love and nature!

His love sleeps on the poet's breast

You can never fathom my love
when you dream on me, breathing now.
I hide you, weeping, pursued
by a voice of steel.

The law that shudders skin or stars
spears my breast
and cloudy words
bite your spirit's wings.

Seven strangers leap into the garden
on horses of light with green manes
hoping to catch your body, my agony.

Shadow me through your sleep.
Hear my blood whirling in violins.
See how they still spy on us!

Night of sleepless love

Us two, with night rising like a moon.
When I started to cry you were laughing:
your contempt a god, my moans
moments and doves chained together.

Us two, with night going, gone. Your weeping
between us a crystal of grief,
my pain a paperweight
sinking through your heart's sand.

Dawn united us on that bed,
our mouths guzzling a winter stream,
its gush blood on our tongues.

Sunlight cut through the shutters
and life's coral opened its branch
over my fading heart.

Last word: an uncollected sonnet

I know that my profile can be calm
in the north of your sky,
its chaste mirror
breaking the pulse of my style.

If ivy and chill linen
are gifts my body bequeaths,
my profile in sand could be the old
steady silence of a crocodile.

Although my tongue of numb doves
will never know the flavour of flame,
only the thorn's bleak hunger,

I'll be an emblem, free from you,
on the neck of a swaying branch
in an ache of dahlias.

Rupert M. Loydell

UNDECIDED

i.m. Ken Smith

Highlight this:
time doesn't happen.
The language sees to that.

I'd like to live the quiet dream,
the quiet and space and order dream,
the white box in the city dream.

There's a breeze this morning
and the temperature's down.
I smell like myself again.

Is that enough certainty for today?
It's all I ever knew or had.
I was working out the implications.

But you? You'll never be sure.

David Hart

ON THE WAY

Year 432 of the Diploma in Experimental Theatre module 1295
moving across the infinite paved Plazas in
silent open discussion of the revolt against the discussion of meaning
cross-referencing the empirical assessment of happenstance while
photographing the unknown in the known then
tearing out the film and feeding it to the pigeons who urge on
the gathering of evidence against meaning, the flooding away of meaning,
the raggedness of impromptu engagement dressing as meaning,
enlightenment exemplified in what most potently has been forgotten,
of creeks, streams, gills, becks, rivulets, brooks, bights and burns,
inferences in the quiet of the soul raging about flow, ooze, seep and
spate, ripple, cascade, trickle, tide, whirl, spate, flood, glide and tears.
We had to be here so as to pass, to say 'Excuse me' and 'Ah' as we pass,
to turn a little and turn back as we pass, to sicken as we pass,
to recover into passing each other and waving across great distance
without intention, to cry out our marks, percentage, assessment, grade,
under the giant lamp of the sun, broken by its light, happening,
accidenting, incidenting, slowly, slowly, in dazed silhouette.

I DID FLOUNDER

I did flounder then, trying to improvise the rules,
if fortunes were to be made this way, with ease
the mind might burn bright blue, like an infant sky.

Anticipation was grey, no-one was here waiting, no guide brought me
directions, no stranger said this is the way.
I thought to offer my heart, thinking the prize a bride,

I heard milk boiling. The day was perfect winter, hard,
pebbly, scarred, wide empty fish in the street floated
around my legs, asking for cash, I said I was a bird

and wasn't believed. For these were not like the days
when a desk was a desk, when coagulants were smiley,
I remembered motionless sheep, no-one was there then, no-one,

and this long after the Almighty had brandished the sun,
had abandoned flickering our eyes and our genitals daily,
had left us – this must be said gently – to our own ways,

and – all the additions now accumulating – simplicty as a prized dream,
and to name it desire, craving,
hunger, longing, yearning, ardour, charged passivity,

walking waist-deep through poppies aching to sing freely.
I floundered then, trying to improvise rules,
there never would be closure, never the true cadence,

anticipation was grey, no-one was here waiting, no guide
around my legs, asking for cash, I said I was a bird
walking waist-deep through poppies aching to sing.

WHILE HE WAS TALKING

While he was talking, the waiter was pushing around a trolley full of cakes,
and, nearly blind, as he talked – the monastery at Chilandari, onion soup,
the walk around the mountain, the view across the Aegean, more onion soup –
his eyes followed the trolley.
Sometimes a secret opens us to itself,
a snowball begins to take shape on a sunny day, just when it's needed,
or a painter falls into a tub of water and emerges blue all over, laughing.

Imagine the trolley full of cakes wheeled briskly along a hospital corridor
and into another, and out of that hospital into another, through the hospitals
of the whole land.
We can live deep even if not for ever, in the present, now,
to be immortal, while in minutes and hours we live, in days and in weeks,
and they pass. I said.
He talked then about the New York City underground,
from Saratoga Avenue all the way to Times Square, then for the fun of it
to Grand Central, changing again to 23rd Street, and couldn't remember why,
and all the while following the cake trolley with his eyes. And paused, surely
to ask for a cream doughnut or a walnut slice, but started on about whelks
and prawns and langoustine.
A fly settled on the table, walked several inches,
scratched itself, looked up at each of us in turn, winked, and flew off again,
and I knew how much older I was, as he spoke of the Saint Matthew Passion
and winter on the mountain, of *seeing* my smile. And began a new walk.

Easy, I said, but he was away. I said, interrupting him, holding his arm,
you could publish this, in cold print, in hot print, on tape, in Braille even,
your wonderful stories. But I knew I was kidding, and he knew it.

Stephen James

TREE FORMS

It could be a spider, it could be a spire,
it could be a tree that shades into a shower.
Still, it's something that you move around,
and try to figure, or sit and stare at
till the shape of it comes clear.

*

A white house – sharp and square and blunt –
with green twining gutters and a blue slate roof
floats free of its frozen field and into the rear-
view mirror, then is over for ever,

but the words for all you've lost still drift beside you,
strung taut like ribbons of tape played
out on branches, or flitting from tree to tree.

*

And in the garden's cold geometry,
where blossom froths and whispers
on latticed frames, you'll surely find
that smile, in full bloom or wilting,
and call to mind once more those hands
unfurling with a gesture of magnolia.

*

Or, again, you'll use that hazy patch of time
when the window's mirror-image on the wall
displays a rippling, cross-hatched square of white
where willow vapours shift and twist and twine
like the sway and snag of thoughts that clarify –
yet leave you feeling sad, or unresolved . . .

*

It could be a tent, or it could be a tower,
it could be a weeping tree made out of hair.

BRIDGE PASSAGES

There's a kind of floating free,
a vaulting of the instep, an uplift
and a shifting of the body-weight
to lighten it.

~

                        Suspension
turns metaphysical, supports itself
by holding you in motion (its framework
but a shimmer in the river).

~

It's as if the bridge gives way
to involution, to glyphs and curves,
and scrolls of frozen latticework,
and scribbles of its meaning on the water.

~

To cross and double-cross the river path,
be drawn into the turbid lull and heave,
to be the stranger on the parallel bridge
who sweeps against the current of your thoughts . . .

~

To be free, to be lonely, to be
pacing out a sentence, as a life,
to look back down along its symmetries,
or grip the rail, and note it as it falls . . .

~

Or to walk back into dreams of treading
over water: you reach out a hand to wave,
to hold, try to bridge the sense of distance
with only the span of your aching arms.

Veronica Gaylie

APOLLO

Man in diapers lies on a mattress
shouting: *God*. Protective undergarment
is the medical term; *God*, the same. Still,
a word drives me through an emergency
waiting room as I make my way to you,
mother, behind a curtain, pale and green,
same colour as my shirt and shorts,
      pale and green, walls and floor.
A cleaning woman calls a breathing machine
a vacuum, *it's called a valve* the nurse says,
as if a word matters while she tugs on a tube
wound close round my mother's neck,
a valve, she repeats, tugs the tube again,
wires and chords, all plugged in, as if
knowing the word *vacuum* means
we are cleaning women.
      We are VCRs, TV sets
      above beds, programmed
      heart and breath.
Curtains are fences where voices lean,
here you hear everything. *Nurse!*
      Someone screams. *Nurse!*
      Someone screams. *Someone needs a nurse!*
      Someone screams. *Stop screaming!*
      The nurse screams.
Ambulance drivers and guards wrestle
an old man with drumstick arms to the ground,
past shaking families, falling bedpans,
a timpani of nurses needing cigarettes
and across a speckled tile Emergency room floor
I see below my mother's curtain,

        someone new,
        a pair of orange suede shoes
        in a sea of pale green so grey
and after tears on a hot stone stoop,
        my world, a green so grey,
        in a fluorescent strain
now a voice so low and sure
without tugging on cords and wires
as if they were attached to answers
no one ever sees. After twelve
hours of questions I watch fingers
touch forehead and cheeks,
lightly, ah, flutter. Couldn't be.
        Eyes dance, TV hangs,
        machine breathes,
a curtain between, pale and green;
now everything rests on orange suede,
a soft shoe. Not a word.

Dawn Wood

REVENGE TRAGEDY

'It locally contains, or heaven, or hell;
there's no third place in't.' – John Webster

It took five years to clear the stage,
to leave only
pillars rising to an arch,
dark walls, running water –

the preoccupations
of drinking, hand-washing;
and a grid fitted to conduct waste
past grained floorboards.

I am frugal. I have saved
few objects – fragments of a mirror;
a book to swear on;
the sweet, delicate fruit he hands her;

curtains to facilitate scene changes
and red, always shades of red.
The floor is tilted forwards severely –
this is why the thin liquid runs –

some from each person – and glints;
although I can't predict
when each rivulet will join or branch
or land in someone else's lap.

Not that any of this is real, of course.
I'm home and lying in this bed, paying
attention to the echoes
of this October debris wrinkling

in a sky that's faintly orange.
As yet, there is no sign of sunrise.

Anne Rouse

HARVEST

There may be red clusters fit for wine,

there may be also:
dry rot, mould, flood-damp,
fire and drought.

The sky can disallow
this stubble of corn,
the winnowed particles of light;
translate the corncrake's rasp
as ragged grieving –

early or late,
none of it
is in your hands.

Alec Finlay

GLAD GOLD

Glenn Gould's
    Goldberg Variations
        Variations

Since you asked
        there was an alluvial
            this morning
the leavings
        of the storm –
            red winter berries
shiny & wind blown
        in the cracks of the paving
            and in the gutter
markings of wind
        and rain.

Glenn Gould, hmmm . . .
        you said   ·
            and I haven't told you
about that piece yet –
        a notation of the hums
            on Gould's *Goldberg Variations* –
the voice preserved
        on magnetic tape
            transcribed as a score
performed on a Steinway
        (model 317)
            cello (solo)
voice (solo)
        and choir.

The *Goldberg* is *nacht music*
        aria & variations –
            little songs without words
played to put
        a King

to sleep.
Gould's performance
    announced a figure
        of artistic genius –
the hums his variations
    on the *Variations*,
        a habit
learned from mother
    his first teacher.

I apologise for
    singing along
        but I would play
less well
    without it . . .
        and for my gestures –
semaphore for sidemen –
    a desire to externalise
        not the music
or even my own
    relation to it
        but perhaps
the responsibility
    for it.

This new score
    gives the listeners ears
        for the barely audible
the alluvials
    that we might call
faith & failure
    gift & wound
        glad & gold.

Goldberg Variations, BWV 988 – J. S. Bach (1742)
Glenn Gould (1955)

Keston Sutherland
HÉROÏDE PASTEL

Coerce the virgin plastic grains it snorts up,
    to scales matched by
it won't ripped like competitors', a tee
    blindfold in crunchy iron—
scurrilous to enamour my walk to
    that parse tree, that you live
off way lined exactly up for a spray
    bullet-points on olive—
in the national gallery of art, Washington
    the statue by Barthélemy Prieur
is 181.5 x 64.3 x 49.2cm, weeps its
    surfactant into a diaper—
it peels away brick-colour, trees that ice
    soil or metal in the busy
flesh are one, with ready doxa laminates,
    pulp to a staggering lonely head.

Erotic grist pinches against its chalk barrier
    wrapping my brain,
you smacked carpet of pâté idea squat tight,
    and the idea is bright—
dishy as fuck, shape of a wing-mirror buried
    in deeply in a slick of
vomited fingernails, mouth which a chunk
    of piss seals—
I can't see any more help they have the
    most amazing doggy bags
except canned, on to its ideal balance-sheet
    scribbled is the plea—
bayonet, uphill back the reflection given
    to my life origin
panto crater keep out of direct
    darkness or drip like fire away.

On the rear of the spine a stencil-drawing
    of an elated baby
wish-list on the scissors themselves is
    is scrawled, be right—
pushes this face off, at rededicate a cinch
    play through the clouded
won't rip it savagely but all civil like glass
    replenished stab-hole—
bits of life crumble from spit on
    screens, licensed
so incendiary what their dispatch thrills
    right to fake ice—
but the sound mirrors the surplus, annuls
    what it's detached
from O Sancta Justitia Bass / Pf racket
    trumpetful of cum.

URGENT REPLY FOR HELP

More than anything it is freedom that I hate
O banality of its disimpaction be remembered
let its indigestible shit-phalanx be on vacation
life insinuated in wicker ice and back-ordered is
by this lovely psychosis more kept up again.

The poll apt to be most rightly reflective
of freedom is incarcerated in the bloodstream
its periodic melos shit administrates, clean out
however of what written in shit itself is
called political significance that blood stutters.

And what is shit, whose own not unusual
disimpaction can ameliorate the posture of him
crouching with his eyes shut, as my love cannot
so shake a blood clot that it reliquefies it
is the perfect regularity of loss traded for need.

Hatred of freedom is not a consequence
of shit per se buttered up to disclose the flip
secrets of its world even to the screaming
baby now dispersed through the cerebellum in sweet
bullet points but is allowed differently.

If you drive three miles the hatred will in
the same time drive seven, likewise in front
of the teeth shit decommissions when my
lips are apart the rupture they propagandize
can fade in its thus futile comparison with hatred.

If this square represents the via negativa
and inside this square there is incarcerated a circle
pinned so it affronts no barrier of the square but
floats in my milky blur of fructose and galactose,
this disbelieved is the unending circulation in love.

Essays

The *Poetry Review* Essay

KARLIEN VAN DEN BEUKEL

Dance

In New York, they think of Edwin Denby as the poet who lifted the embargo on the sonnet. They think of his sonnets as "lighting up from within with a kind of Mallarméan lucidity".

His actual body seems to have done so too.

His neighbours on West 21st Street called him "the man next door who radiates light". The poet Frank O'Hara imagined his step approximating European architecture, or dance:

> Embarcadero, aren't you
> dying to see him in a
> white suit, as a friend saw him once
> in Italy, a white shoe
> nearing the Spanish Steps?

Jacob Burckhardt remembered how Edwin Denby was once spotted on the subway by a posse of black youths who encircled him, chanting "white man, white man" as he stood quite still.

> Desire makes our
> enchanter gracious, and
> naturally he's surprised to
> be. And so are you to be
> you, when he smiles.

It's one of those facts that if you were educated at Dalcroze's Institute of Eurythmic Dance, as Denby was in 1923, you got the neuro-muscular capacity to radiate light all your life. People unabashedly noted his luminosity, flirting with him in the streets and on public transport, and in poems.

It can also become a hagiographic matter, radiance, in certain milieus.

"He was small, old, handsome, pale as an ivory crucifix", the novelist Edmund White remembers. "He almost never spoke, but when he did he whispered. His dignity and beauty and attendance at almost every performance of Balanchine's company symbolised the role that that particular organization had played in New York's intellectual and cultural life since the 1950s."

If his distinction, here too, was to be an icon, it was because he had enlightened people about dance.

Denby's dance critical reviews, published in *Modern Music, The New York Herald Tribune* and *Ballet* from the 1930s and 1940s onwards, had already been collected in *Looking at the Dance* in 1949. Regarded as one of the most influential critical works of the century, it allowed the dance – both modern and ballet – to become central in the postwar cultural ascendancy of New York. Not only did Denby register contemporaneous choreographies with a lucid elegance that continues to establish reputations, even today, but he invented a discourse for an art form that, because of its material transience and indeed its contested status as art form, had evaded proper critical appreciation.

The New York poets remember going to the dance with Edwin Denby. They remember talking with him after in the streets, in fluorescent diners, in the subway, and in his loft. They did not just attend the ballet at the State Theater, but also modern dance performances by young choreographers in downtown venues, as Frank O' Hara wittily recalls in his poem "Dances before the Wall".

Denby's ideas on art, then, were mediated through the social activity of looking at dance. He influenced both the first generation of New York poets, in particular Frank O'Hara and James Schuyler, both of whom he first met in 1952, but also the second generation, poets like Bill Berkson, Ron Padgett, Alice Notley and Ted Berrigan. His dance writing – especially the later collection of essays, *Dancers, Buildings and People in the Streets* (1965) – could be read as a pleasurable handbook to New York School poetics. As Denby remarked on dance writing: "If it succeeds in attracting poets – it should be for a century or so to come fun to write and read". Even so, it is proper to recognise that the writing's intellectual sensibility comes out of a response to its subject, dance. Denby's own visualisation of his body in public space gives us the measure of his critical project.

"The critic's social value", writes Denby in 1949, "is that of a man standing on a street corner talking so intently about his subject that he doesn't realize how peculiar he looks doing it. The intentness of his interest makes people who don't know what he's talking about believe that whatever it is, it must be real somehow – that the art of dancing must be a real thing to some people some of the time. That educates citizens who didn't know it and cheers up those who do".

II

Denby, first of all, wants to make people believe dance is "a real thing" in society. His is not a theorised position; in other words, he does not conceptualise the social real through psychoanalysis or Marxism, as did many 1930s modern dance intellectuals. Nor is he interested, as were the 1930s ballet critics, who stood in partisan conflict with the modern dance lot, in validating the ballet as the only transcendent dance form through New Criticism, so arguing for an inexorable line of aesthetic progress through which an exclusionary Western classical dance canon is established.

Writing on all kinds of dance in an apparently casual American idiom, Denby illustrates its technical principles with examples of physical activity in everyday life, sport, popular film and social occasions. He is thus unconcerned with defining its status as an art through authoritative critical discourse, which he regards as "a fiction like that of a sea-serpent". His social real is based on the physical experience of daily life, from domestic rituals to strolling in city streets, as well as the awareness that these ordinary movements are subtly different in different places, culturally determined:

> Daily life is wonderfully full of things to see. Not only people's movements, but the objects around them, the shape of the rooms they live in, the ornaments architects make around windows and door, the peculiar ways buildings end in the air, the water tanks, the fantastic differences in their street facade on the first floor.

Denby's comment on the nineteenth-century Romantic ballet critic and poet, Théophile Gautier, applies to his own work too: "Art for him is not a temple of humanity one enters with a reverent exaltation. Art is a familiar pleasure and Gautier assumes that one strolls through the world of art as familiarly as one strolls through Paris".

In strolling around cities, Denby is interested in observing how everyday movement informs dancing, even classical ballet. Ballet technique, or *danse d'ecole*, aims to achieve an ideal standard of classicism, beyond place, which is why ballet critics call it a transcendent aesthetic. That is not, however, how Denby looks at it:

How different the more consciously social movements are – coming into a room at a party, shaking hands, behaving at table, or sitting in a chair – everybody knows from foreign movies anyway. Dancers who grow up in a city naturally move in the way people around them have moved all their life. And that makes a difference in the overall or general look of a whole company, even if it doesn't show in one dancer doing a particular step. But classicism is so naked and enlarged a way of moving that any tiny unconscious residue in it of something else than the step – the residue of habit or of character – shows.

Ballet companies reveal their integral relation to their particular cities, and thus to culture, through the dancers' bodies. Denby is interested in the cultural differences that are unconsciously revealed in ballet technique. His reviews of the Bolshoi, the New York City Ballet, the Royal Ballet and the Paris Opera, attempt to identify in their style, traces of habitual conduct in their cities. He invites us to consider the relation between place and the dance, between social performance and art performance.

Calling Balanchine ballets "dance entertainments meant to be watched by the natives of New York", he mocks the ballet critics, but perhaps also the potential seriousness of his own cultural ideas. "Ballet is absurd by nature. But its absurdities are civilised ones." Often he will retreat, make light of it, as if intellectualising would negate its meaning.

And perhaps it does. The very fact that the ballet has not quite managed to transcend common social reality, that the "tiny unconscious residues of habit" still show up in its aesthetic discipline, is its meaning as art: "A faint reminiscence of a gesture seen with wonder as a child and long forgotten, an overtone characteristic of a city in the motion of someone one has loved and forgotten, returns sometimes in a dancer's innocent motion and makes its poignancy the more irresistible".

We know the involuntary memory cannot be accessed through rational intellect. Dance – I think it must also be because it is immediately sensuous – allows access to the forgotten. It is a subjective experience but within the shared domain of culture. To Denby, then, the formalised movement of ballet can bring to light the forgotten Gestalt, allowing ineluctable reminiscences of past experience to come into play.

"Art takes what in life is an accidental pleasure and tries to repeat and prolong it."

III

Denby, secondly, wants to make people believe dance is "a real thing" as art work.

Collected by friends after the ballet, Balanchine's *The Four Temperaments* performed by the Royal Ballet, I tried making them believe I had seen "a real thing". I could only clearly remember one particularly vicious passage, and that I had to illustrate by marking the steps on the pavement outside Covent Garden.

To have recalled in words the immanent material complexity of the abstract ballet variations, so that my friends could experience being immersed in its imaginary realm, and then to indicate how it mattered as art, was beyond me.

Denby writes the dance performance in action. At its finest, his dance writing has the build-up, pacing, and concentration of live sports commentary:

> What one enjoys most in reading is the illusion of being present at a performance, of watching with an unusually active interest and seeing unexpected possibilities take place.

Somehow, his writing is able to give that experiential sense of dance. You can visualise exactly what is going on, as here in Balanchine's *Concerto Barocco*:

> Then at the culminating phrase, from her greatest height he very slowly lowers her. You watch her body slowly descend, her foot and her leg pointing stiffly downwards, till her toe reaches the floor and she rests her full weight at last on this single sharp point and pauses. It is the effect at that moment of a deliberate and powerful plunge into a wound, and the emotion of it answers strangely to the musical stress.

Seeing how the movement works out may come more quickly to a trained dancer than to the rest of us. It is Denby's writing, however, that gives access to the emotional complexity of that movement. The unassuming, but incredibly confident language choices – for example, to use the present tense, to take ordinary words to describe classical technique, to arrange the syntax so that the pertinent image has an after-shock as it would have if one was seeing it performed – project dance as a real-time event, immediately there. Moreover, we know from the writing that this dance is art.

Frank O'Hara believes that sensitivity to the performative possibilities of language is at the heart of Denby's writing:

> This idea, I think is the basis of Denby's prose and poetry, a style which "demands a constant attention to details which the public is not meant to notice, which only professionals spot, so unemphatic do they remain in performance." He was speaking of ballet performance, but the idea is equally true of Denby's writing performance, and one of the important secrets of its pleasures.

If Denby's writing performance is like ballet performance, then however effortless it may appear, it must have its own basis in literary discipline. "It is hardly by chance", notes Lincoln Kirstein, the founder of the modernist literary journal *Hound and Horn* and the New York City Ballet, "that the most thorough writers concerned with dance were prime poets – Théophile Gautier, Stéphane Mallarmé, Paul Valéry. Other verse makers who observed dancing with some attention, but are rarely read for it, are Frederico García Lorca and Hart Crane. It is to these master choreographers of words that Denby is most akin".

Lincoln Kirstein sees Denby's work as connected into a symbolist-modernist genealogy of dance poetics with its lyric scions in New York. To Kirstein, the authority of Denby's dance writing comes from its relation to the modernist poetry tradition. Indeed, Kirstein adroitly canonises Denby's dance writing: "His prose is textbook information, chapter and verse".

Both as a dancer and a poet, Denby was educated in an avant-garde modernism strongly associated with women exponents: by the Institute of Eurythmic Dance, where both Marie Rambert and Mary Wigman had studied and taught, by magazines like *Transition*, and by the work of Gertrude Stein, whom he considered "our greatest living poet".

Certainly, Mallarmé's idea that the dance can be given virtual presence through the performative nature of poetic writing, through syntax, rhythm and typographic positioning, informs the many extraordinary dance poems of the modernist period. The idea also informs Denby's critical working method: "To give in words the illusion of watching dancers as they create a ballet in action requires a literary gift. An abstruse sentence by Mallarmé, the rhythmic subtlety of a paragraph by Marianne Moore, a witty page-long collage of technical terms by Goncourt, can give the reader a sharper sense of what dancing is about than a book by an untalented writer, no matter how much better acquainted with his subject he is".

In Denby's critical practice, poetic writing has an integral function in giving "the illusion of watching dancers as they create a ballet in action". Poetic writing – an attention to the possibilities of grammar, rhythm, and visual features – is not a lyric flight from criticism, rather it establishes the critical subject, the dance as a real thing.

IV

The New York poets were Denby's first public as a poet, or rather, they first made his poems public. His first collection, *In Public, In Private*, was published in 1948, followed by *Mediterranean Cities* in 1958. Later, Ted Berrigan published a collection of his sonnets in a special edition of "C" magazine in 1963 with an Andy Warhol silkscreen of Denby on the cover. Anne Waldman and Ron Padgett published his *Collected Poems* in 1975. The *Complete Poems*, edited and introduced by Ron Padgett, was posthumously published by Random House, New York in 1986.

His sonnets are compacted, recalcitrant. A lot of people are thrown, at first, by what seems to be an awkwardness in his sonnets, dissonant bits that become all the more pronounced because of the formal poetic structure. Ron Padgett remarked that at first he thought that Denby's poems were "inept (like saying Jackson Pollock is messy)".

Denby's sonnets are mainly about everyday routines in cities. Their imaginative scope is entirely determined by the surroundings they are about, by being in a particular place. The sonnet – it flows, then not, a rhythmic obstacle, a word, an elision, gets in the way, or opens up a new direction. I imagine these linguistic effects like a kerb or a button. These usually unnoticed things in daily life can turn into felicitous props for lovers, proud feats for children, frustrations for the old. In Denby's sonnets, complicated modalities arise through seemingly ordinary details of poetic language, the tension between rhythm and meaning, line and sense, word and word order. I imagine that his poems could be read proprioceptively too, that the poetic language can suggest the subtle orientation of body in place. He reads other people's work carefully, alert to language practice, as he mentioned in an interview toward the end of his life:

> Recently I was reading a collection of poems and felt a sudden shift, which at first I couldn't identify. In a very modest, unemphatic way a simple "it" had been slipped in which had the effect of changing the whole sense of the four lines before and the three or four lines which followed. In just one sentence everything had been changed as a result of the placement of one two-letter word. You enjoyed the feel of that, sensed the correctness. The same is true of the shifts in Balanchine's dances. As subtle as they may be, they are essential to the life and meaning of his work.

Denby's dance writing does not elucidate the subject matter of his poems, but it does, perhaps, the poetics of his sonnets. But the poem is not a dance. You can read it here, now (or later). You can put it in your pocket. You can show the entire thing to others. You can read it again. Here is a Denby poem.

V

Roar drowns the reproach, facing him
Quite near, subway platform, she heeds
Head tossing slow like a pony's
In the wrong, the pinto I rode
A boy of twelve, that lovely head
Quarrels I believed riders win
White-haired pass these lovers in luck
Hurry to ballet, its invention
Where there's no quarrel, but there's fate
A scream unhurried of music's choice
And we recognize the games played
Like in heaven, foreknowing they cease
The move, the pitch arrive, turn to air
Here, as if love had said forever.

Unhappy, strange conglomerate

MARK FORD

Thomas Lovell Beddoes, *Death's Jest-Book* (The 1829 Text),
ed. Michael Bradshaw, FyfieldBooks, £9.95, ISBN 1887545990
Thomas Lovell Beddoes, *Death's Jest-Book*
(A new edition of the later text established by H.W. Donner),
ed. Alan Halsey, West House Books in association with
the Thomas Lovell Beddoes Society, £14.95, ISBN 1904052088

Last year was the bicentenary of the birth of Thomas Lovell Beddoes, one of the most peculiar, haunting, and prodigiously gifted English poets of the nineteenth century. Beddoes published only two books in his lifetime: *The Improvisatore* (1821), a collection of Gothic tales in verse, and *The Brides' Tragedy* (1822), a pseudo-Jacobean drama that was widely praised by reviewers, and even prompted the odd favorable comparison with Shakespeare and Marlowe. But Beddoes set little store by these juvenilia – indeed he was so ashamed of *The Improvisatore* that he took to buying up all the copies he could find and destroying them; if he noticed the volume on a friend's bookshelf, he would surreptitiously remove its pages with a razor, and then return the empty binding.

Beddoes's dissatisfaction with his own work is one of the most striking features of his self-aborting literary career. Between 1823–1825 he embarked on four separate verse dramas – *The Last Man*, *Love's Arrow Poisoned*, *Torrismond*, and *The Second Brother*. Many of the scenes and fragments that survive from these are quite superb; consider, for instance this preternaturally vivid passage from *The Last Man* describing an adult and baby crocodile:

> Hard by the lilied Nile I saw
> A duskish river-dragon stretched along,
> The brown habergeon of his limbs enamelled
> With sanguine almandines and rainy pearl:
> And on his back there lay a young one sleeping,
> No bigger than a mouse; with eyes like beads,
> And a small fragment of its speckled egg
> Remaining on its harmless, pulpy snout;
> A thing to laugh at, as it gaped to catch
> The baulking merry flies. In the iron jaws
> Of the great devil-beast, like a pale soul

Fluttering in rocky hell, lightsomely flew
A snowy trochilus, with roseate beak
Tearing the hairy leeches from his throat.

In the summer of 1825, however, on the eve of his departure from England to study medicine at the University of Göttingen in Germany, Beddoes wrote to his friend Thomas Forbes Kelsall with news of yet another projected verse drama, "a very Gothic-styled tragedy, for which I have a jewel of a name – DEATH'S JESTBOOK". In it he planned to approach the problem that motivated both his medical researches, which centered on anatomy, and his imagination: for Beddoes the "only truth worth demonstrating" was the exact nature of death.

This obsession may have had its origins in his early years. Beddoes's father, the polymathic Dr Thomas Beddoes, was a political radical, a poet, and a scientist: expelled from his readership at Oxford because of his republican sympathies during the French Revolution, he settled in Bristol where he became friends with Coleridge and Southey, composed an unreadable verse epic, *Alexander's Expedition down the Hydaspes and the Indus to the Indian Ocean*, and co-founded the Pneumatic Institution with James Watt and Josiah Wedgewood. Dr Beddoes believed that children should be inducted into the mysteries of birth and death as early as possible. Accordingly, the Beddoes offspring were made to witness "the labour pangs of a domestic quadruped", and to participate in the dissection of pregnant frogs and hens. Thomas Lovell was only five and a half when his father died in 1808, but his life, like the Doctor's, was to be divided between medicine, radical politics, and poetry.

Beddoes was firmly convinced that "the dramatist & physician are closely, almost inseparably allied"; dissecting and writing were both ways of probing the secrets of death, and possibly of discovering, in a quest that resembled that of another Romantic "modern Prometheus", Mary Shelley's Victor Frankenstein, the origins of life also:

And even as there is a round dry grain
In a plant's skeleton, which being buried
Can raise the herb's green body up again;
So is there such in man, a seed-shaped bone,
Aldabaron, called by the Hebrews Luz,
Which, being laid into the ground, will bear
After three thousand years the grass of flesh,
The bloody, soul-possessed weed called man.

This speech is given in *Death's Jest-Book* to Ziba, a necromantic Moor

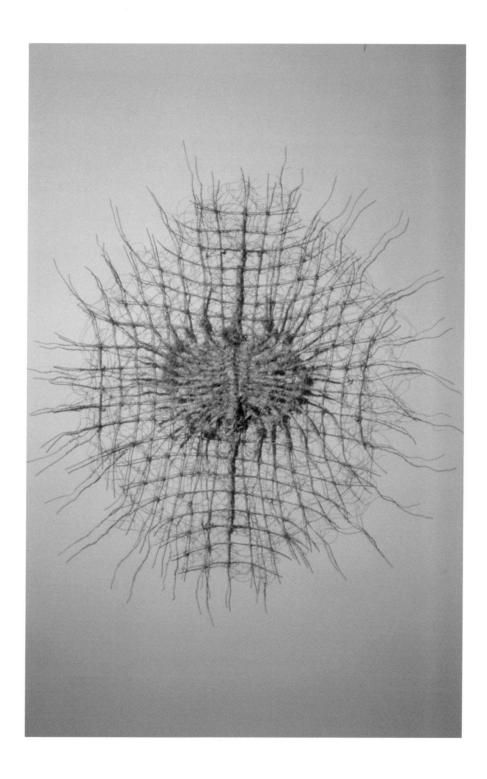

who is about to raise a ghost from the grave – as it turns out, the wrong one – but is supported by a long note by Beddoes himself in which he quotes Talmudic texts relating to this mystical bone, "the only one which withstands dissolution after death, out of which the body will be developed at the resurrection".

Beddoes was fascinated by the hinterland between here and after, by ways of representing the transition between life and death – and vice versa. In a passage of couplets composed for this scene, but eventually cut, he sardonically imagines a body poised for resurrection:

> Thread the nerves through the right holes,
> Get out of my bones, you wormy souls,
> Shut up my stomach, the ribs are full:
> Muscles be steady and ready to pull.
> Heart and artery merrily shake
> And eyelid go up, for we're going to wake.

But the theme also inspired some of his most magically lyrical and subtle effects, as in the fragment from *The Last Man* that pictures a corpse "Turning to daisies gently in the grave", or the fantasy of recovered love momentarily indulged in Beddoes's best-known poem, "Dream Pedlary":

> If there are ghosts to raise,
> > What shall I call,
> Out of hell's murky haze,
> > Heaven's blue hall?
> Raise my loved longlost boy
> To lead me to his joy.
> > There are no ghosts to raise;
> > Out of death lead no ways;
> > > Vain is the call.

"Dream Pedlary" was composed in 1830 in the wake of Beddoes's first attempt at suicide. In 1827 he had met an impoverished Jew called Bernard Reich, from whom, or so he claims in his note, he first learned of the Hebrew belief in the bone Luz. Beddoes and Reich shared lodgings in Göttingen in 1827 and 1828, and moved together to Würzburg in the autumn of 1829. Reich then abruptly vanishes from the record: he may, as Beddoes's first biographer, H.W. Donner has speculated, have died, but the conjecture is based more on the desire to identify the "loved longlost boy" of "Dream Pedlary" than on hard evidence. It does seem certain, however, that the disappearance or loss of

Reich compounded a crisis in Beddoes's literary career, a crisis from which, in a sense, he never recovered.

Beddoes dispatched what has come to be known as the 1829 version of *Death's Jest-Book* in February of that year to three friends in England; the heroically loyal Thomas Forbes Kelsall, a solicitor based in Southampton, Bryan Waller Procter (who himself wrote faux-Jacobean plays under the pseudonym Barry Cornwall), and the novelist and poet J. G. H. Bourne. While the ever-supportive Kelsall was all for immediate publication, Procter and Bourne strongly counselled Beddoes to embark on root-and-branch revision. "Am I right in supposing", Beddoes wrote in response to Procter (whose original letter does not survive), "that you would denounce, and order to be rewritten, all the prose scenes and passages? – almost all the 1st and 2nd, great part of the 3rd act, much of the principal scenes of the 4th, and the 5th to be strengthened and its opportunities better worked on? But you see this is no trifle, though I believe it ought to be done." Procter's and Bourne's advice was effectively to imprison Beddoes in the ghoulish, labyrinthine world of *Death's Jest-Book* for the rest of his life. He ended up spending the next two decades emending and expanding his masterpiece, rewriting speeches, adding lyrics, tinkering with names, and complicating still further the plot of what he aptly called, in 1844, his "unhappy, strange conglomerate". "What good", expostulated Robert Browning, one of Beddoes's greatest admirers, in a letter to Kelsall of 1868, "was got by suppressing the poem, or what harm could have followed the publication even in the worldly way of looking at things? Suppose it had been laughed, blackguarded in Blackwood, fallen flat from the press? The worse for the world for the quarter of an hour: Beddoes would not have much cared, but probably made a clean breast and begun on something else. It is infinitely regrettable."

Beddoes himself freely acknowledged the defects in his play – indeed seems always to have been witheringly critical of his own abilities. He confesses that the "power of drawing character & humour – two things absolutely indispensable for a good dramatist – are the two first articles in my deficiencies". It's true that all the characters in *Death's Jest-Book*, and in all of Beddoes's other verse dramas, speak the same gorgeous literary fustian. What kind of poet, Ezra Pound wondered in an essay of 1913, might Beddoes have been had he "used a real speech instead of a language which may have been used on the early Victorian stage, but certainly had no existence in the life of his era?" Yet Pound, like Browning, found himself enthralled by the extraordinary delicacy, verve, sweep and intelligence with which Beddoes energizes his literary imaginings. Beddoes's *oeuvre* – and in this again it resembles Frankenstein's monster – seems made up of dislocated fragments dug up from the past, uneasily stitched together, then suddenly galvanized into an unnerving, startling life. "What is the lobster's tune when he is boiled?" demands Death's principal jester, Isbrand, by way of introduction to a song which, he explains, he "made / One night a-strewing poison for the rats / In the kitchen corner":

> Squats on a toad-stool under a tree
>   A bodiless childfull of life in the gloom,
> Crying with frog voice, 'What shall I be?
> Poor unborn ghost, for my mother killed me
>   Scarcely alive in her wicked womb.
> What shall I be? shall I creep to the egg
> That's cracking asunder yonder by Nile,
>   And with eighteen toes,
>   And a snuff-taking nose,
>   Make an Egyptian crocodile?'

Something of the homelessness of this "childfull of life in the gloom" permeates Beddoes's singular poetic sensibility, as it sifts through archaic literary idioms, fitfully animating the properties it borrows from the traditions of the grotesque, the tragic, and the sublime. As Pound declared in *Canto LXXX*, Beddoes is truly "the prince of morticians".

Beddoes's characters are all, as Lytton Strachey remarked in a wonderful essay of 1907, "hypochondriac philosophers, puzzling over eternity and dissecting the attributes of death". The plot of *Death's Jest-Book*, even in its original simpler version of 1829, is hard to summarize concisely. Set in Ancona, Egypt, and Grüssau in the late 13th (1829) or 14th (later text) century, it involves betrayal, revenge, love-rivalry, conspiracy, revolution, fratricide, and sorcery. The play opens with an expedition led by the noble Wolfram to rescue the Duke of Münsterberg, Melveric, who has been taken captive by "wild pagans" on a pilgrimage to the Holy Land. Although Wolfram knows Melveric murdered his father, he has not only forgiven him this, but the pair have entered into a pact of blood-brothership. Wolfram's real brother, Isbrand, at this point the court-jester, is not so "womanish", and vows to revenge his father and usurp the dukedom. In Egypt, meanwhile, Melveric has fallen in love with one Sybilla, who is herself in love with Wolfram, with whom she had once shared a cell during an earlier captivity. Wolfram rescues both, but is then heartlessly murdered by the ungrateful Duke. Wolfram's body is shipped home for burial, but is smuggled by Isbrand into the vault containing the remains of Melveric's ex-wife, so when Ziba performs his spell, it is the ghost of his murdered friend rather than that of his saintly spouse that emerges from the tomb.

An equally elaborate line of action concerns the Duke's two sons, Adalmar and Athulf, who are both in love with the same woman, Amala. Although betrothed to the warrior-like Adalmar, she secretly loves the satirical and licentious Athulf. On the night before the wedding, Athulf drinks what he thinks to be a fatal vial of poison, confesses his love, which, thinking he is about to die, she reciprocates; but the poison, provided by the all-purpose Ziba, turns out to be merely an opiate. On discovery of this, Athulf, proclaiming "Now that I live, I will live . . . Away to Abel's grave!", murders Adalmar, only to be overwhelmed immediately by a terrible remorse, imagining himself, in a typically Beddoesian flight of fancy, transformed into

> A wild old wicked mountain in the sea:
> And the abhorred conscience of this murder,
> Shall be created and become a Lion
> All alone in the darkness of my spirit,
> And lair him in my caves
> And when I lie tremendous in the billows,
> Murderers, and men half ghosts, stricken with madness,
> Will come to live upon my rugged sides,
> Die, and be buried in it.

That same night Isbrand's conspiracy, which has been infiltrated by the Duke himself, disguised as a pilgrim, comes to a head and sparks off the general mayhem with which the play climaxes. Beddoes's commitment to radical politics emerges in the curious character of Mario, an allegorical embodiment of the spirit of revolution who – although blind – manages to stab Isbrand ("Down, thou usurper, to the earth and grovel!") at the moment of his seeming triumph. The play's concluding image is of the Duke being dragged alive into the world of the dead by Wolfram, his mild-mannered ghostly nemesis. Both versions also feature a set of prose-speaking grotesques with names like Titmouse or Homunculus Mandrake who offer somewhat laboured Jonsonian light relief, and are studded – particularly the later one – with exquisite songs and macabre lyrics that delay still further the inching progress of the convoluted action.

"Just now," Beddoes observed in a letter of 1825, "the drama is a haunted ruin". It could be awakened only by "a bold trampling fellow – no creeper into wormholes – no reviser even – however good. These reanimations are vampire-cold". But far from reinvigorating the contemporary stage – which was dominated by the vogue for the pseudo-Jacobean – as he seems to have planned, Beddoes devoted his extraordinary talents to what is essentially an agonizingly prolonged dissolution of the genre of verse drama, a kind of unending kiss of death, an ultimate and literal enactment of the crisis he had diagnosed. Like his own ghostly "Phantom-Wooer", Beddoes seems like a spectre enticing his chosen medium into oblivion:

> A ghost, that loved a lady fair,
> Ever in the starry air
>   Of midnight at her pillow stood;
> And, with a sweetness skies above
> The luring words of human love,
>   Her soul the phantom wooed.
> Sweet and sweet is their poisoned note,
> The little snakes of silver throat,
> In mossy skulls that nest and lie,
> Ever singing 'die, oh, die.'

Death's Jest-Book became itself the "haunted ruin" to end all haunted ruins, one Beddoes could neither complete nor abandon. It is both unperformable, and, as he himself pointed out, "perfectly adapted to remain unread". Yet, from another perspective, *Death's Jest-Book* is a startlingly prescient work, one that anticipates not only the dramatic monologue, as developed by Tennyson and Browning – a point first made by Christopher Ricks – but the black humorous worlds of such as Samuel Beckett or Ionesco. And in its conflicted, doomed, self-defeating form, at once fragmentary and endlessly expansive, it now seems the perfect expression of Beddoes's vision of "the absurdity and unsatisfactory nature of human life".

Beddoes's own life ended particularly unsatisfactorily. Expelled from Würzburg for his incendiary political views and speeches, he settled for awhile in Zurich, then drifted on to Berlin then Baden then Frankfurt, where he met

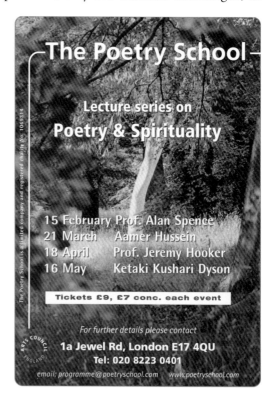

Konrad Degen, an aspiring actor, but professional baker, who was to be his companion for the last years of his life. Beddoes also took to making occasional trips to England, or Cantland, as he called it. During one of these in 1846, in protest at the poor state of the English theatre, he attempted to burn down Drury Lane by lighting a £5 note and holding it underneath a chair. He was never an entirely welcome guest at the family seat at Cheney Longville, for he refused to meet fellow guests or talk to his hosts; once he arrived drunk astride a donkey, and spent the entire six month visit that followed alone in his room, smoking and drinking.

Beddoes's lawyer, Revell Phillips, was convinced his second suicide attempt in 1848 was due to a "love disappointment". While staying at the Cigogne Hotel in Basle he cut open an artery in his left leg. He was admitted to the Basle Hospital, where he kept tearing off the bandages in the hope he might bleed to death. Eventually the leg had to be amputated. Beddoes remained in the hospital until on January 26th of 1849, he was found dead with a suicide note addressed to his lawyer on his chest. "My dear Phillips", it began, "I am food for what I am good for – worms". He instructs his only consistent admirer, Thomas Forbes Kelsall to go through his manuscripts and "print or not as he thinks fit". "I ought to have been", Beddoes continues, "among other things a good poet. Life was too great a bore on one peg [a reference to the amputation] and that a bad one. Buy for Dr Ecklin [Beddoes's doctor at the hospital] above mentioned [one of] Reade's best stomach pumps". Beddoes, it later transpired, had taken poison, although it has never been established exactly how he obtained it. The stomach pump he bequeathed his physician, therefore, was Beddoes's final jest with death; since Dr Ecklin would only receive it on the poet's decease, it could never be used to clear his own system of the poison he had deliberately taken. One can't help imagining him murmuring, as he approached the threshold he had addressed in so many soaring monologues and mournful dirges, the chorus of his final lyric:

> Sweet and sweet is their poisoned note,
> The little snakes of silver throat,
> In mossy skulls that nest and lie,
> Ever singing 'die, oh, die.'

Beside himself

PETER McDONALD

Robert Lowell, *Collected Poems*, Frank Bidart and David Gewanter (eds), Faber, £40, ISBN 0571163408

Towards the end of *History* (1973), Robert Lowell sets up a particular reading of his career – one provided already, conveniently enough, by a disapproving critic:

> Ah the swift vanishing of my older
> generation – the deaths, suicide, madness
> of Roethke, Berryman, Jarrell and Lowell,
> "the last the most discouraging of all
> surviving to dissipate Lord Weary's Castle
> and nine subsequent useful poems
> in the seedy grandiloquence of Notebook."

Quotation can be deadly; sometimes, it can be deadly for all concerned. Here, the words quoted are from Donald Hall, who had written about the "self-serving journalism" of Lowell's *Notebook* (1970) in a 1972 issue of the *Review*. Ending Lowell's sonnet as they do, Hall's words have their vulnerability laid bare: the prissy exactness of "nine subsequent useful poems" (which nine? and "useful" to whom, or for what?) is not cruelly, but justly exposed in the process of quotation. One effect of all this is to make the grand critical overview itself seem a vanity – one in line with Hall's own vanity, in this case – which the creative energy of poetry itself cannot stop for or entertain. And yet, Lowell's sense of *oeuvre* is not really put aside here, any more than Hall's faulty view of it is ignored: there is a career to be considered, and even the white-heat of Lowell's early 1970s creativity knows it. In the context of "deaths, suicide, madness", thoughts of an *oeuvre* are already shadowed by mortality, and a book like *History* (itself a rearrangement and augmentation of poetry published earlier) might be less a re-animation than a dressing-up of something dead and gone. As the first line of Lowell's sonnet asks, "Is dying harder than being already dead?"

One phrase of Hall's which does not have its sting removed or reversed in Lowell's quotation is "seedy grandiloquence". We might say that, since *History* in a sense abolishes its predecessor volume, or at least replaces it, Lowell is able to show the steps taken to root out the seedy and grandiloquent in *Notebook*'s verse; but it would be harder to demonstrate either his seriousness or his success in such a project. In fact, "seedy grandiloquence" is so pointed and cutting because it goes to the very core of more than *Notebook*, and touches a raw nerve close to the heart of all Lowell's poetry. From the beginning, Lowell's natural mode was undeniably grandiloquent – though grandiloquence, in itself, can hardly count automatically as a vice in poetry. But "seedy" does something serious to "grandiloquence", and its pitch of disapproval seems to draw on all kinds of areas in Lowell's career: the hint of a New England aristocrat gone to seed, the suggestion of something improper and vaguely disreputable behind all the high style, and perhaps an allusion to the disquiet surrounding the poet's enlistment (by 1973, indeed, a press-ganging) of his private life to creative duty.

The Lowell *oeuvre*, whatever its degree of grandiloquence, is certainly one executed on a grand scale: but more than half of the 850-odd pages allocated to Lowell's published collections in the *Complete Poems* are taken up with work from the last ten years of the poet's life, and there is inevitably a sense in which the later, prolific Lowell tends to overbalance the work as a whole. To compound matters, it is of course this later Lowell whose art takes for its subject the life – and the life's work – of the artist himself. The trio of volumes, made in 1973 from unrhymed sonnets old, remodelled, and new (*History, For Lizzie and Harriet, The Dolphin*), occupy between them more than 280 pages, and it is in these books above all that Lowell battens on his own life with the same appetite he had earlier shown for his times, ensuring that autobiography physically outweighs everything else in the *oeuvre*. *Life Studies*, Lowell's outstandingly brilliant (and artistically consequential) volume of 1959, might have seemed to the poet to underwrite the explosion of self-scrutiny which the verse of *Notebook* and after constitutes; but this is not obviously the case, and the shimmering (often, in fact, autobiographically elusive) artistry of *Life Studies* might be seen as a sharp contrast to the large-scale, impetuous and uncensored exposure of the later sonnets. At worst, this is something more than "seedy", for Lowell was ready to let others as well as himself suffer for his art. In her impassioned review of *The Dolphin* in 1973, Adrienne Rich (once a pupil of Lowell's) quoted from that book's last poem as an example of "bullshit eloquence":

> I have sat and listened to too many
> words of the collaborating muse,
> and plotted perhaps too freely with my life,
> not avoiding injury to others,
> not avoiding injury to myself –
> to ask compassion … this book, half fiction,

an eelnet made by man for the eel fighting –
my eyes have seen what my hand did.

For Rich, this was "a poor excuse for a cruel and shallow book"; she pointed out that "it is presumptuous to balance injury done to others with injury done to myself", and (referring to Lowell's inclusion of lines from his ex-wife's letters and calls) concluded that "the same unproportioned ego that was capable of this act is damagingly at work in all three of Lowell's books". Certainly, a book owning up to being "half fiction" may be presumed to be half fact, and the failure to say which is which is a definite "injury to others" which it does not take much moral integrity to avoid. But an ego out of proportion, and without any sense of right proportion, is the inescapable subject of later Lowell, so much so that it lays claim to the earlier work too, as though the megalomaniac, rampaging, occasionally out-of-control speaker of the 1973 sonnets were consuming it, bloated with his own sense of an *oeuvre* and a self that have become indistinguishable.

The impact of Lowell's 1973 publishing binge, and the difficult issues stirred up by it, are perhaps still such as to push critical perspectives out of their just proportion. And it has not been possible, until now, to see the Lowell *oeuvre* easily in its complete form. With the poet dead for more than a quarter of a century, the particular kind of corpus represented by a *Collected Poems* is late in appearing, and it would doubtless have been better for everybody to have had this book, or something like it, long ago. Nevertheless, the effect of putting all of the poet's individual volumes together (with the exception of *Notebook*, represented only through the subsequent revisions and developments of the 1973 books) is to make palpable, and compelling, the case for Lowell's status as a major mid-twentieth-century poet. Despite his own (and his critics') worst efforts, there is much more to Robert Lowell than his ego: indeed, the range of work which he produced goes to show how complex, fraught, and deeply-impacted an element for that ego Lowell's poetry actually, and always, was. From the beginning, Lowell's creative strength both needed and made for itself a drama of form: the ways in which metre – the rhythms of lines, the comings and goings of sound, the demands and revelations of rhyme – perform their own transformations on the writing self (or, as it necessarily also is, the speaking voice), and make that self part of a larger drama, are essential to Lowell's response to the lyric impetus. One consequence of this is that Lowell's poetry is able to accommodate a self which, in terms of biographical circumstance, was of exceptional and far-reaching historical interest. The *Collected Poems* gives permanent form to a voice uneasily – often violently – at odds with the imperial culture from the heart of which it speaks, and for which it finds the forms of dramatic speech capable of fusing public with private agonies.

It is important to insist on the dramatic element. Writing on his own work in the last year of his life, Lowell took time to dwell on Browning's example and importance:

> The large poet of the nineteenth century who attracts and repels us is Robert Browning. Who couldn't he use, Napoleon III, St. John, Cardinal Manning, Caliban? He set them in a thousand metres. Nor was his ear deficient . . . . And yet Browning's idiosyncratic robustness scratches us, and often his metrical acrobatics are too good. One wishes one could more often see him plain . . . . Yet perhaps Browning's major poems will outlast much major fiction. Meanwhile he shames poets with the varied human beings he could scan, the generosity of his ventriloquism.

These are not the words of a writer who has, in any straightforward sense, given up on "ventriloquism" in favour of seeing the self "plain": for the cannily gentle-humoured tone of Browning's "Memorabilia" ("And did you once see Shelley plain?") is being enlisted here to suggest the centrality of the dramatic to the ways poets might imagine, and see, themselves. And do we then see Lowell plain? *History*'s opening sonnet gives one kind of answer:

> As in our Bibles, white-faced, predatory,
> the beautiful, mist-drunken hunter's moon ascends –
> a child could give it a face: two holes, two holes,
> my eyes, my mouth, between them a skull's no-nose –
> O there's a terrifying innocence in my face
> drenched with the silver salvage of the mornfrost.

Amongst other things, lines such as these show how "idiosyncratic robustness scratches us" in Lowell's verse: just as the penultimate line is irritated by the excess of "terrifying" (four syllables, where the ear expects two), so the entire medium for this attempt at self-regard proves more robust and troubling than simple reflection would warrant. How "predatory" is the face – not, in the end, the moon's – which emerges here? Like the speaker of a Browning monologue, Lowell is surprised, or pulled up short, by a self his own words have brought to light. And the poet's ear – like Browning's, very far from "deficient" – makes shocks like these all the more true and troubling.

"Waking in the Blue" (from *Life Studies*) ends on another self-portrait, also tinged with ventriloquism:

After a hearty New England breakfast,
I weigh two hundred pounds
this morning. Cock of the walk,
I strut in my turtle-necked French sailor's jersey
before the metal shaving mirrors,
and see the shaky future grow familiar
in the pinched, indigenous faces
of these thoroughbred mental cases,
twice my age and half my weight.
We are all old-timers,
each of us holds a locked razor.

Those "metal shaving mirrors" offer no very comforting reflections – indeed, they seem instead to project a future in which Lowell's line, like Banquo's in *Macbeth*, might stretch out to the crack of doom – but as a stricken parody of the "indigenous" and "thoroughbred" in New England history and culture which Lowell himself all too surely embodies. But this is not just – or even primarily – a matter of imagery: the stanza brilliantly makes real a "shaky" state in which statement, like perception, finds itself compromised by a circumstantial force. Recovery is in question even as it attempts to announce itself (the difference between "I weigh two hundred pounds this morning" and "I weigh two hundred pounds/ this morning" is unnervingly arbitrary, but unmistakably real); rhyme inveigles and insinuates itself, as "indigenous faces"/ "mental cases" returns in ghostly form with "locked razor" – "a final rhyme", as Ian Hamilton observed, "superbly softened, inexact and ominous". What verse like this ventriloquises is the order – a kind of determinism, perhaps – ready to impose itself on the given, individual life which perceives only the disordered and disordering world of sickness and distress; and it is not exactly good news. In grandiose terms (but then, with Lowell, the grandiose is sometimes an unavoidable register), the personal is shaped – and crippled, tortured, possibly in the end destroyed – by the history in which "We are all old-timers".

The phases of Lowell's poetic career embody a number of different discoveries of this central fact. Throughout, however, the artifice of verse and the dramatic meanings (or liabilities) of form are the necessary elements and preconditions of those discoveries. In the high polish of *Lord Weary's Castle* (1946), Lowell demonstrated a convincing mastery of the wrought and anxiously rhetorical lyric line, which is freighted with all kinds of literary influences, from Shakespeare and Milton to Hopkins, Allen Tate, Auden and Dylan Thomas, but which nevertheless succeeds here, more often than it has any right to do, in producing poetry of overwhelming originality and power.

These early poems are dramatic events, but what their ornate, rather baroque formal medium ventriloquises is often in excess of what Lowell, as a young and ambitious writer, can fully reflect on or understand. As pointedly Roman Catholic as it is New England, Lowell's voice in self-conscious revolt produces lyric intensity, but perplexes itself in attempts at statement, risking everything instead on gestures of (often apocalyptic) significance. It is Lowell's formal element in *Lord Weary's Castle* which cannot find the words to address the world (or, perhaps, to address Robert Lowell) with an answerable clarity.

The development into the dramatic monologue, explicitly Browningesque in design and execution, in Lowell's second collection, *The Mills of the Kavanaughs* (1951), was indicative of the poet's growing awareness of the dramatic dynamics in poetic form. In "Falling asleep over the Aeneid", the volume's outstanding poem, the poet inhabits the voice of "an old man in Concord" – an old man with a Lowell pedigree – who finds himself ventriloquising the voice of Virgil's Aeneas at the funeral of Pallas, his Italian ally, who has been a victim of the wars following the Trojan invasion. The perspectives are dizzying: empires, as Lowell had shown earlier in poems such as "At the Indian killer's grave", are founded on land-grab and massacre, and to read the *Aeneid* from the centre (in this case an aged, forgetful and powerless one) of New England political culture is to engage in a fundamental questioning of power and historical fate. The old man's vivid dream-life is (at least as he reads it) one conducted inside an imperial master-text of conquest and destiny. As a dramatic monologue, the poem is able to harness a terrible force of fantasy, as when the old man speaks for Aeneas, surrounded by bird-priests at Pallas' funeral:

> Left foot, right foot, as they turn,
> More pyres are rising: armored horses, bronze,
> And gagged Italians, who must file by ones
> Across the bitter river, when my thumb
> Tightens into their wind-pipes. The beaks drum;
> Their headman's cow-horned death's-head bites its tongue,
> And stiffens …

The sharp actuality of the violence here – something accepted uncomplicatedly by the old man/Aeneas speaker – is being controlled and directed by the dynamics of the dramatic monologue itself. So, the ornate, muscle-bound line "Their headman's cow-horned death's-head bites its tongue", which has all the noise and impacted energy of a line from *Lord Weary's Castle*, is now as much symptom as it is a performance: the lesson, like the movement of the couplets themselves, is something learned well from Browning. In Lowell's hands, this enables a complex staging of imperial thought and circumstance, and results in a startling realisation of the violence in, or behind, even the harmlessly antique. The poem does not tell its readers what to make of this – for the dramatic monologue can do no such thing; instead, it makes the issue real through compelling speech.

In *Life Studies*, Lowell was able to make use of autobiography as part of the dramatic whole – now, of course, a delicately-structured one, in which one poem could glance off another, and last words, or definitive conclusions of any kind, would be put in a state of indefinite postponement. At the same time, the volume is also a series of definitive acts of self-recognition (which, as Lowell shows, self-dramatisation does not preclude); the poet encounters himself again and again, learning more (and differently) each time about himself and his culture. In a way, after the high religious temperatures of the earlier work, *Life Studies* is Lowell's discovery of his own inner Protestant – poetic form is the element of self-detachment here, and there is a calm, rather than an impassioned, embrace of history's meaning for an individual. History, now, is something far more involved and subtle than before. Instead of apocalyptic anticipation, the continually unravelling and reconstructing self of *Life Studies* toils in a state of the perpetually unfinished – self-knowledge is never complete, or likely to be completed.

At his best, Lowell finds ways of making the self, conceived in this way, meaningfully resonant in the context of both history and the contemporary world. In his two major volumes of the 1960s, *For the Union Dead* (1964) and *Near the Ocean* (1967), Lowell achieved what very few English language poets of his century could manage, and wrote a public poetry of real solidity and resonance. Again, this seems to have been, at least in part, an instance of Lowell's voice growing into the authority of its own formal capacities, discovering the confidence of a public voice in the battered integrity of an examined self. In the Marvellian stanzas of some of *Near the Ocean*, Lowell created something distinctly new by allowing the form itself so completely to possess his own voice. The lines are not the servile exercise of a pastiche, but Marvell in Lowell's true voice; having learned already, in *Imitations* (1961), the creative possibilities of balancing the original and the inherited, and how, in acts of poetic translation, the faithful and the faithless have to co-exist, Lowell was able to absorb Marvell's tetrameter couplets so fully that he could bring them to meaningful contemporary life. In "Waking early Sunday morning" this issues in extraordinary poetry:

> When will we see Him face to face?
> Each day, He shines through darker glass.
> In this small town where everything

is known, I see His vanishing
emblems, His white spire and flag-
pole sticking out above the fog,
like old white china doorknobs, sad,
slight, useless things to calm the mad.

The counterpoint here between rhythm and phrasing is that of a virtuoso, but the poignancy of the stanza derives from a painfully exposed and vulnerable perspective; as the imagery of divine knowledge and providence recedes, so the pace changes, and the rhythmic surroundings, with their wayward delivery of rhyme-words, adjust to accommodate a world miserably provided for. The equable tone – which is transmitted directly from Marvell – is pointedly inscrutable; for Lowell's purposes, it accommodates (but does not calm) a contemporary reality in which all the power left to the individual conscience resides in its particularity of perspective.

Lowell's strongest public poetry does not denounce empire from a distance, like some prophet in the wilderness; instead, it speaks from within the social and historical structures of power, and talks through the madness at the core of imperial ambition and imagination. Obviously, there are attendant dangers in this description, as there were very actual dangers for Lowell, since it brings into proximity the mental afflictions of an individual with the spiritual distresses and delusions of a whole culture: who is to tell these apart, and how? And it is the late second half of Lowell's poetic career, the enormous blank sonnet-sequence of *Notebook* and the 1973 volumes, which makes such dangers especially real. The question for any critic of Lowell's completed *oeuvre* is how far the author manages to avoid mere "grandiloquence" in coping with the self as part of the drama of poetic form, a drama which is by the time of the later work completely inseparable from historical imagination. It is important – though it is also very difficult – to separate this question from issues of ethical or moral evaluation. The worth of Lowell's writing is greater than the worthiness of his life; but this is something which the poet in him knew, and it is to his credit (not just, perhaps, his artistic credit) that he trusted in the artifice of verse to let so many difficult truths – about himself, certainly, but about the world also – be spoken.

The *Collected Poems* has all the copiousness and fecundity of a major poet, and it presents a body of work which – despite all the sound and fury of Lowell's constantly accelerating life – feels curiously complete. The last volume, *Day by Day* (1977), is a delicate epilogue to something achieved and over; in this respect, its tentative (sometimes meandering) free verse seems fittingly informal and detached. A good epigraph for Lowell's work might be a reversal of the familiar Latin tag to read *ars brevis, vita longa:* art is short, and life is long. There is a concision to Lowell's art, a sometimes reckless decisiveness to his powers, which gives it a quality of unanswerable finish; as for life, Lowell knew only too well that it does not imitate art in that regard. The first lines of *History* are as sombre an opening to an epic as can be imagined:

> History has to live with what was here,
> clutching and close to fumbling all we had –
> it is so dull and gruesome how we die,
> unlike writing, life never finishes.

This is ominous news for us as men and women, perhaps, but necessary knowledge for poets. Like his great Victorian predecessor, Lowell knew what it meant to put faith in poetry to take in as much as possible of the world, with its unfinished lives and histories, and to "set them in a thousand metres".

Reviews

How new is new?

Andrew Duncan, *The Failure of Conservatism in Modern British Poetry*,
Salt, £16.95, ISBN 1876857579

Here's a contentious, contradictory, controversial book I want to
defend despite its defects and contend with despite its virtues. Some
of it has me standing up and saying, "Yes Yes". Some of it makes me
want to go out for a long walk to clear my head. Sometimes I have these
responses to two adjacent sentences. A lot of people will oscillate between the
same reactions, but for many different reasons.

Duncan surveys what he sees as the "alternative" British poetry decade by
decade from the 1950s on, making lists of poets he believes important and
interesting, and of what he sees as the main poetic fashions, preoccupations
and obsessions at various moments. He focuses mainly on poetry in England
and attempts explorations of Wales and Scotland, though not Ireland. Dotted
through the book are discussions of particular poets he wants to praise or
spurn. Some poets get fairly detailed and sympathetic interpretations, some a
pillocking, some a name-drop or two. Aside from this, there are forays into
various topics: for example, how (negatively) he thinks others perceive the
English (pp. 1-5); his versions of theories about how poetic style changes (pp.
10-22); his list of thirty-four features indicating modernist technique (pp. 36-
44); his notions on structure of consciousness and personality (183-190); his
takes on the politics of the '80s and (mainly French) "theory" (pp. 233-239),
on feminism and poetry (pp. 148 ff and 239 ff), on poetry and the age of
information (pp. 243-252). And much more. These forays aren't "digressions":
through them, he aims to illustrate points about language, culture and art, all
of which he treats, and at all times in relation to politics,

So this survey of fifty years of poetry is ambitious. At first sighting,
Duncan's scope seems admirable, as do his breadth of reading and reference,
his curiosity and inquisitiveness, his zest and energy. There's a great deal of
closely researched information, and there are hundreds of insights, some
fascinating, some way-out, some precious, abstruse and recondite, into
nexuses of British poetic activity, many of which are hardly known outside
their own circles of practitioners and advocates. Duncan is immensely knowl-
edgeable and has immersed himself in his subject: he lives it. Even though
there are very few poets he appears to respect and like unreservedly, when he's
dealing with one whose work he does have some sympathy with or affection
for, he can drop himself into a text, submit to it, let it work on him and, in this
way, serve as a helpful and informative guide, tossing out hints about possible

ways of reading, especially when meanings don't yield themselves all that easily. He's capable of suspending the need for prefabricated ordering principles and containment mechanisms, and of taking off into a text on trust, to find out what it may have offered up by the time he gets to the end, retrospectively.

Even so, this isn't meant to be an objective study and the book in no way attempts a systematic-scholarly survey of all the turbulent and multi-directional (overlapping, coalescing, diverging, etc.) currents and threads in British poetry over the last fifty years. From an editorial point of view, it must be said that the book's presentation is so scrappy and disorganised, and its index so rudimentary and haphazard, as to be infuriating. But apart from the fact that Duncan states a disrespect for literary academics anyway, he's also a man with an active mission: to revise the established canon and advocate an alternative poetics; and these two strands get twisted into a polemic at times fascinating, coherent, open-minded and persuasive, occasionally brilliant in swift and unexpected insights and enthusiasms, and at times narrow, doctrinaire, prejudiced and embittered.

🖋

Duncan's main contention is that, regardless of minor shifts and oscillations, the pattern of power structures in the British poetry world that have held sway throughout the last fifty years still appears to be in place today. There's a lot in this argument and it's a fascinating field. He argues that there does exist a recognisable range of approved styles, poems, tones of voices and blends of attitudes that make poets eligible for Mainstream/Establishment status. The considerable task he sets himself is to attempt to identify and analyse the implicit criteria that govern the rules of inclusion (approval, acceptability, admission, etc.) and exclusion (disapproval, dismissal, rejection, etc.), both of which usually get expressed in terms of "editorial decisions" on "quality" and "suitability". From the outset he draws his lines clearly and the tone is combative:

> . . . maybe British society, or a certain subdivision of it called the culture industry, has been hostile to new poets and crushed the life out of them; reducing them to paranoia; forcing them to do other work to make a living; forcing them to write in conventional or light modes or go unpublished. Part of this could be due to excessive love for dead writers . . . Excessive love for the past leaves less psychological space for thinking about the future; at the worst, this makes you become a scholar, forking

over the creativity of the past, and abandoning and suppressing your own creativity. Pastiche and antiquarianism are national characteristics, as well as being neuroses.

Then, consider this:

> This country has been too long the huge second-hand market. We want to get rid of the countless museums which smother it with countless graveyards. Do you want to waste the best part of your strength in some pointless admiration of the past, from which you'll only emerge drained, diminished, trampled on? ... Daily visits to museums, libraries and academies (those grave-yards of wasted effort, calvaries of crucified dreams, registers of false starts!) are for artists what prolonged supervision by par-ents is for intelligent young men ... The oldest among us aren't yet thirty.

This second quote comes from Marinetti's Futurist manifesto (1909): I've changed the first word from "Italy" to "This country". Closer juxtaposition shows almost astonishing similarities in patterning of thought:

1. Italy ... the huge second-hand market (M); British society, or a certain subdivision of it called the culture industry ... pastiche and antiquarianism (D).
2. pointless admiration of the past (M); excessive love for dead writers ... excessive love for the past (D).
3. artists ... intelligent young men ... The oldest among us aren't yet thirty (M); hostile to new poets (D).
4. waste the best part of your strength ... only emerge drained, diminished, trampled on (M); crushed the life out of them; reducing them to paranoia (D).
5. countless museums ... smother it with countless grave-yards ... museums, libraries and academies ... grave-yards of wasted effort, calvaries of crucified dreams, registers of false starts (M); become a scholar, forking over the creativity of the past, and abandoning and suppressing your own creativity ... pastiche and antiquarianism ... national characteristics ... neuroses (D).

So, here's a good question: is Duncan's book any more than a rehashing of the clichés of modernism, but with an updated set of names? In the light of this comparison, any claim that Duncan's preoccupations are new or original seems dubious; and whether his analysis is anything like accurate let alone subtle enough to deal with a very different situation, ninety-four years after Marinetti, must be equally open to doubt. Clearly, the deeper conceptual and historical issues reopened by this book are to do with the *structure and nature of the avant-garde itself.* Most of Duncan's failings, as well as some of his strengths, stem from his involvement in pretty predictable avant-garde positions and polemics.

✍

Duncan's other main area of interest concerns *pleasure* and *anxiety*, and the contradictory ways in which these connect with ethical and political values. Duncan challenges what he sees as a "rule that that the poet has to be grim and clenched up". So back to the biggest *bête noire* of all:

> I am unclear what the reader is supposed to do with the poems of Philip Larkin . . . What a creeping depression and lowness of spirits seeps out of his work. Larkin precisely defines what poetry should not be: poetry is exciting, Larkin is depressing; poetry is hyperassociative, Larkin discourages the formation of ideas; poetry is emotional, Larkin is frigid and prudent; poetry is social, Larkin dislikes other people; poetry takes risks, Larkin cringes.

Whatever one thinks of this evaluation, it does provide the best entry into the more solid aspects of Duncan's argument, which are exemplified in the incontrovertible fact that the dominance and popularity of Larkin in the contemporary Anglo-Saxon imagination, and of poets like him or influenced by him (as evidenced by anthologies, biographies, critical studies, insertion into syllabuses and, most recently, a TV play), do indeed provide clear indications of a whole set of dismissive and negative attitudes towards kinds of poetry that try to set up *different* expectations, possibilities, ways of thinking, feeling, experiencing, being. In its crudest form and without the much needed qualifications and contradictions which Duncan does in fact provide (and in considerable detail, decade by decade), the further gist of the argument is that, during most of the second half of the twentieth century, certain groups of not-very-good poets, usually in their capacity as editors, have grabbed and kept the central stage in English poetry by means of a series of concerted and successful ongoing bids to publish their equally-not-very-good associates, and so have rigorously kept out more talented and interesting poets who don't conform to the normative models these editors have had vested interests in perpetuating. These editors, and the poets they publish, together with the styles they approve and perpetuate, are the elements Duncan classifies, condemns and caricatures as "conservative". Although this blanket use of the political term is hugely over-simplified, made to cover a multitude of sins and obviously needs much fuller and clearer critical analysis, it's at least interestingly provocative and lays down an open challenge that deserves answering. The argument continues: that this kind of editorial cronyism has resulted in decades of mediocrity at the centres of literary power, and the purveying by these centres of meretricious and perniciously false images of what is "valuable" rather than what is truly good and bright and alive in British poetry, which is to be found hidden at the peripheries and in the margins. This too may be a bit simple-minded, but it has more than a dollop of truth in it.

*

The list of poets Duncan pits against what he sees as the "conservative" mainstream is rich and large. Among many others, it includes: Ian Hamilton Finlay, W. S. Graham, Ted Hughes, Charles Tomlinson, Geoffrey Hill (with reservations), Edwin Morgan, Iain Crichton Smith, Christopher Middleton, Flora Garry, Kenneth White, George MacBeth, Roy Fisher, Rosemary Tonks, Peter Redgrove, Penelope Shuttle, J. H. Prynne (who receives the most discussion), John James, Ken Smith, Denise Riley, Allen Fisher, Tom Raworth, Barry MacSweeney, Jeremy Reed, Jeffrey Wainwright, David Harsent, Walter Perrie, Kelvin Corcoran, Isobel Thrilling, John Ash and Ulli Freer.

Aside from the fact that there are many fine poets unrecognised in Establishment circles whose names *aren't* included or, if so, aren't fully recognised by Duncan, this is nonetheless a broad if oddly idiosyncratic list. Well, why not? We could all supply our own equally personalised alternatives. Duncan's rambling and untidy notes aren't intended to be an exclusive or authoritative catalogue anyway. What's more interesting here, though, is that there's obviously *no identifiable aesthetic (poetic) or ideological (political) common factor*, not even that of "anti-conservatism", to bond all these poets together. In terms of Duncan's central argument about conservatism, then, his list certainly makes very little theoretical sense; and so goes a long way to illustrating, and perhaps proving a point of his own: that the modern Anglo-Saxons, Duncan included, aren't much good at, or particularly interested in, *theory*. As for *quality*, Duncan is hardly adept at offering samples: among poems he quotes I found only a few lines (notably by J. H. Prynne, John James, Ken Smith and W. N. Herbert) which invited further

reading, in terms of finesse in movement of thought and feeling, linguistic orginality and strength, and/or intellectual depth, beauty or passion. And not only that: some of the poets he lists are no less uninteresting than many of the middle-of-the-road Establishment poets he refuses to consider on account of their so-called "conservativism". Mediocrity is no more confinable than cronyism or corruption. Furthermore, by contrast, several poets in his list have never turned far from the limelight or steered even slightly off-course away from a safe and well-plumbed mainstream; and, although some of these are "good" poets by any account, they can hardly be thought of as *alternative*, *experimental* or *avant-garde* by any stretch of the imagination. In particular, consider Ted Hughes. None of these "radical" labels fits him at all. Hughes was always the darling of the Establishment: "discovered" as a Cambridge under-graduate; published by Faber; traditional rural conservative; poet laureate; supporter of hunting, royalty and the landed gentry; beloved of what Duncan calls "the heritage-and-culture-industry"; fancied for his rugged, tragically flawed, mesmerising, "animalistic", Heathcliffian persona – a familiar and well-documented stereotype; far more interested in myth and magic than in "ideas" or intellectual debate; and as far as his verse is concerned, less of a stylistic experimenter or innovator than a powerful and original but wholly traditional wordsmith. (And apart from all this, if Hughes, then why on earth not Plath?) In the face of what Duncan describes as the "island prejudice against intelligence in art" and "the distaste in Britain for speculative philosophy", the book repeatedly argues for a poetry of articulate enquiry, radical intellectual challenge and philosophical content. I think he's correct to take this line against philistinism or barbarism. But are any such qualities to be found in Hughes? Like many other features in his book, puzzlingly, infuriat-ingly, it just doesn't add up.

🖊

Duncan does get round to confronting some of these contradictions in a section subtitled "Two Sublimes", even though not very satisfactorily. Here he offsets tendencies which he represents by Robert Graves, Peter Redgrove and Ted Hughes against those he sees in W. S. Graham and J. H. Prynne. Although I've reservations about the accuracy of his statement with respect to at least two of these individual poets, the remarks in themselves are interesting, for here indeed is a hint that Duncan may be beginning, blurrily, to glimpse patterns and perspectives outside his own conceptual frames:

> The intellectual faction has a queasy sensitivity about: metaphor, appropriation; feelings; projection; myth;

spirituality; love. The inability to identify makes it impossible to
write about other people.

Does this signal Duncan moving towards a more subtle theory? That's too early to tell. But what is clear is that, until this point, precisely his own prejudices about the avant-garde have been his blinkers. Seeming not to have grasped that poetic activity inside the UK doesn't operate in terms of a two-party system, and that the conflicts he rages about are almost the same as those of the Group and Movement versus Dylan Thomas, Duncan consistently misrepresents diversity by reducing it to opposition between "conservative" and "non-conservative". Reflecting a peculiarly British insularity, and perhaps an underlying British puritanism too, his oppositionalist mental structure itself systemically blocks or limits understanding. Incidentally, there's scarcely a single mention throughout the book of any poet outside the UK. Shades of his own *bête noire*, the xenophobic Larkin?

There's no getting away from it: if taken in unadulterated form, Duncan's two-toned theory is completely inadequate to distinguish poems of really high calibre, let alone greatness; nor is it likely to predict or generate their making. It's true that many poets on his list of favourites are very fine indeed and deserve a much better deal. However, their quality is certainly not definable or even approachable *just* in terms of "conservatism" or "radicalism" but is, rather, to do both with matters of fine textual detail and larger factors like love, depth, originality, insight, compassion, imagination, inspiration, craft, gift and freedom. There must be sympathy with Duncan's rage; and attention is needed to the areas he has opened up. But there's now more than ever an urgent call for a poetics embodying generosity, magnanimity, hospitality and inclusiveness, to generate works that move way beyond his parameters.

Despite all its contradictions, flaws and drawbacks, and regardless of whether one agrees with his analysis or not, Duncan's work is exciting, original, valuable and full of fascinations, enthusiasms and energy. It *bounds with life and hope*. The first thing it deserves is to be debated, and the very last, cold-shouldered. Duncan has a busy, active, provocative mind; and there's such a wealth of stimulating, controversial and topical material here that it can't easily be ignored or dismissed except by those with vested interests of their own to hide. There are bound to be many such people on both (or, rather, all) sides. He deserves maximum praise and credit for (at least) two further reasons. Firstly, he's fully opened up areas for debate that are relevant to all poets writing in the UK today, that everyone involved in poetry in the UK knows about, and that most poets spend a good deal of time *thinking* about, but most find difficult, and even embarrassing or frightening, to *talk* about – because doing so might involve exposure of areas of chronic anxiety.

Secondly, the issues he has broached are wider and deeper than the actual scope of his book itself. Duncan's untidy, headlong, often feckless, reckless candour makes interesting work possible on a wider, more inclusive and more magnanimous scale than his own set of references allows. The book helps us chart and understand a little of what we've come through and where we may (be able to) go. In these respects, it's to be seen as a brave, honourable, single-handed achievement.

RICHARD BURNS

Antique lands

Peter Didsbury, *Scenes From a Long Sleep: New and Selected Poems*, Bloodaxe, £10.95, ISBN 1852246081

This ample book reintroduces a poet of versatile intelligence and exceptional linguistic range: Didsbury's scenic lyrics, quizzical meditations, verse-letters, vignettes, opprobria, and historical impersonations offer an attractive personality and a plenitude of wonderful lines, but surprisingly few perfected poems.

Scenes begins with forty-three new poems, then covers his three previous volumes in reverse chronological order, ending with *The Butchers of Hull* (1982). Didsbury's readers have rightly looked not just to his Humberside locale for keys to his poetry, but to his longtime profession, archaeology, whose attitudes and values the poetry shares: patience, respect for all artifacts (especially the trivial), interest in how the past informs the present, suspicion of grand schemes, attention to each detail. One good poem takes place "in the claylands, / where archaeologists get what they deserve" and "the County Council pastures its yellow snow ploughs."

Didsbury's characters often act like archaeologists: when he admires them, they are careful diviners; when pitiable, or ineffective, they are lost eccentrics, malingering in a half-ghostly middle England. Didsbury himself, poet-as-archeologist, can do well with pure description, making strange the overfamiliar. An "iron pail" is "Blanched in historical cement"; a tuba (perhaps from a military band) "seems to be gulping light from the snow,/ trying to rid its mouth of the taste of warplanes." Conversely, the poems keep conclusions (his and ours) tentative, subordinate to the details which produced them. A "leaf / at the end of Janet Maccombich's prayer book" reveals

a simple sum;
some hastily scribbled words (milk? Thursday?);
and a careful sketch of the face of a cat
peering out of dense foliage,
or perhaps with wings intended to be innumerable.

Angel? Mouser? Doodle? (Are you sure?) Such passages do well to depict confusion, unsureness, lasting bafflement at the ambiguous evidence which makes up the world.

Didsbury's linguistic choices also imply an archaeologist's values: he cherishes rare finds, obsolescent constructions, Latinate or specialized vocabulary. A winter storm leaves behind "chiliocosms of snowflakes"; in "The Coffin Factory", "offcuts of veneer . . . slither" through "our semi-industrial suburb", reminding the poet of "land-adapted conger eels", then of Constantius' "vicennial advent into Rome". His rhythms place the complex subordinations of 18th and 19th century English prose into modern free verse: "that which is swallowed in our recursive ginnel / is that which is excreted". Often Didsbury appears to be tacitly quoting, to adapt sources even when none is in evidence: he does well to impersonate not speakers but writers, both famous (Laurence Sterne) and obscure (Janet Maccombich).

Didsbury's aptitudes also fuel epigrams: "Our lives are short, / and those who taught us have died". His poems resemble letters and essays, histories and landscapes, rather than sculptures or creatures or songs; in geological terms they are not igneous, nor metamorphic, but sedimentary, accreted from independent bits. One poem even calls itself an "Ode to Broken Thoughts – like broken biscuits, / shaken in a tin on an open hand". Many of Didsbury's lines, but few of his poems, seem inevitable, finished, unable to be other than as they are. The poet often lets five fine lines stand where two would do; many poems could lose, or gain, several sentences without much effect on the shape of the whole. In his single best poem, "The Smart Chair", Didsbury's propensity to go on for too long acquires force in itself: we extemporize and chatter and speechify (the poem suggests) as if to postpone death.

That idea might remind you of Hull's most famous poet, and Didsbury might not mind: far behind their detailed (or cluttered) surfaces, the poems can reveal a clear, sad, Larkinesque core. "I am promised my death, and the rest will / take care of itself," one poem muses; in another, corpselike outdoor sleepers (or are they sleeper-like corpses?) lie like "two hands of cards disposed . . . face down upon the turf, / as if in the expectation of return." Like Larkin, Didsbury wants a metaphysics, but not badly enough to adopt one. "Theological problems," he writes, "now . . . make me tired, as one is tired by a child"; instead, his "world of phenomena gathers at the surface / of a system of unity powered by emptiness". Didsbury's historical researches, and his alienated stoicism, might also remind you of Peter Reading. Like Reading and Larkin, Didsbury enjoys dysphemisms and flytings, "farting and belching across the puddle boards." But Didsbury deploys a stethoscope and a mallet where Reading would use a jackhammer, and Didsbury actually seems to like other people (however distant from them he sometimes feels).

"We are not suited to the long perspectives," Larkin wrote, but Didsbury is suited to those above all. "The Classical Farm" regards with Horatian equanimity the burning of a school; "Antique Lands" sees Blair and Thatcher and Disraeli as reincarnations of Ozymandias. An earlier poem "record[s]… joy" that "Men have lived. Even so far from us, / in place and time as this". The worst thing about Didsbury's work is its diffuseness, its low ratio of forests to trees: the best thing is its respect for its own intelligence, its refusal to simplify, streamline or talk down. The last of the new poems ends, "That which I stood and watched did not require / me in any way to adopt a different posture." Of course not: Didsbury's virtues, and some of his vices, grow from his ability to see middle England as if it were ancient Sumeria, a strange land whose fascinating ways he details and contemplates, but cannot change.

STEPHEN BURT

The spirit of a shaggy dog

Don Paterson, *Landing Light*,
Faber, £12.99, ISBN 0571219934

Is it Francis Ponge or François Aussemain who said "The bed sees us add ourselves to the world, then subtract ourselves from it"? No, it's not that master of the modern prose-poem, Ponge, it is in fact Aussemain, Don Paterson's Francophone alter ego, the convincing near-forgery who briefly reappears in this new collection. The quotation here – it goes on in this entertaining and rather beautiful fashion for over nine lines of lyrical prose – is from an epigraph to the continuation of Paterson's now long poem "The Alexandrian Library", early appearances having occured in previous books. That poem, except for the Aussemain quotation, is reading rather tiredly now, as if it can't escape from its own Borgesian fractals, and perhaps, now that it has reached the point of triptych, it is time for it to be laid to one side; maybe in preparation, if it survives reflection, for a booklet or fine press publication in its own right.

This is an unsettled collection: sequentially awkward (although miscellenea have their place, too), and even technically rough-and-ready at times. There are, for example, the rhymes Paterson contrives for his translation of Dante's thirteenth canto of the *Inferno*: amongst them, "razor-clawed" with "tortured"; "tearing me" and "hearing me"; "of this hell" and "is so incredible". Perhaps these and others can be read as para-rhyme, suitably harsh for a poem about the pains of hell. I certainly like the cheekiness of rhyming "which I unlocked" with "heard no click" – there really does seem considerable thought behind that rhyme as it is so obviously muted (remembering the deadlock of –ck, and pushing the "d" back into the centre of the line) – but the translation as a whole does not always feel so deliberately misshapen.

This is not, of course, to fault the ambition. And translations are always in some sense a new work. The ambiguity over whether Paterson's Machado-inspired collection *The Eyes* is being marketed as more Paterson than Machado is unwisely resurrected in the note to *Landing Light*, which describes *The Eyes* as one of the Scottish poet's "three" collections, and Machado is again uncredited. With this brought to mind, some readers will find the number of translations in this new book (Dante, Rilke, Cavafy), while they seem fine in themselves, cause for the nagging thought that a publishing treadmill is being trundled here and that translations are one way of keeping supply up. The poem "'96" suggests a writer's block thankfully evaded – "no poem / all year / but its dumb // inverse / sow's ear / silk purse – but the collection as a whole feels transitional, a struggle for both poet and reader.

There are advantages to the unsettled. Paterson's use of a Scots in some of the poems here is confident, derived ultimately from Hugh MacDiarmid's imagistic interwar experiments, but learning from the disconcerting viewpoints in W. N. Herbert's more recent Scots texts, too. The lines "Lass, they say / oor nation's nae / words for love / the wiy we have / for daith, or deil", from "Twinflooer", revisit an already very much visited part of the Scottish literary landscape – the relationship between the Scots language, Scottish nationhood, and the capacity to express emotion – seeming to lyricise it away from Herbert's jagged "Forked Tongue" to something more botanical, before re-introducing harshness with the image of the double flower "nailed thegither / wame to wame" [belly to belly].

The Scots language is available for other tones besides this kind of near-reverential disgust (and the trope of self-disgust?), but even Paterson's English language poems, the great majority of this collection, seldom fully escape it. A variant, however, is grim humour, as in the set-piece "St Brides: Sea Mail", in which an islander reports the extinction of the local bird, whose carcass has been traditionally used as an airworthy model aeroplane. The nod to Douglas

Dunn's "St Kilda's Parliament" is decidely jocular – perhaps parliamentary democracy is a glancing rather than a deliberate target ("The last morning / we shuffled out for parliament / their rock was empty"), but this poem is probably more in the spirit of a shaggy dog story than anything else. There are a number of other poems of that kind, and the reader might feel that, to change metaphors, there is actually more propulsion in these poems than there is aeroplane. A few of the shorter, more concentrated pieces, are the most memorable ones for me. The enigmatic six-liner "America", despite its seemingly portentous title, and its Patersonian interest in the grimmer aspects of the body, matches the impossible abstraction of naming a country with the physical facts of the anatomy – here, a drowned man "turned and curled and [...] boked up" by the sea – before collapsing ideal and fact away from each other: "then came apart and fell into the surf". It is a sullen highlight in a book which only raises expectations for the next collection.

RICHARD PRICE

Lyric flight

Medbh McGuckian, *Had I a Thousand Lives*,
Gallery, £7.99, ISBN 1852353465

A t the very least, *Had I a Thousand Lives* challenges the charge that Medbh McGuckian's poetry is "apolitical". A memorial to the executions of the Irish radicals, Robert Emmet and Thomas Russell, the collection explores the power of speech and the uncertainty of Irish identity against the recent cease-fires in the North. The title is taken from a speech made by Russell in October 1803, and the collection bears traces of his international perspective conveyed by the ballad about him, "The Man From God Knows Where". An itinerant who witnessed the wrongs of English colonialism across the globe, Russell's aim was to "unite Irishmen of all religious persuasions".

Drawing on the power of oratory and song (the "breath-poem" and "mouth music") throughout, the collection includes a poem about the terrain of "Slieve Gallion" in Co. Derry; a poem which makes reference to "Slieve Gallion Brae", a traditional lyric mourning the exile of Irishmen abroad. Throughout, the political is entwined with the natural world and there are a number of poems about birds and bird-song, including "The Rock Dove", "Photograph of a Passerine in Song" and "Porzana Porzana". This is possibly a gesture towards Seamus Heaney's "Sweeney" poems, and these are echoed by images of flight and exile central to McGuckian's understanding of Irish identity. The cover picture, by Antrim born artist Basil Blackshaw, connects with Heaney's cover page to "Sweeney Astray", as it depicts a "Bird on a Wire", a fitting perch for the poet addressing the precarious politics of Ireland present and past. In view of this, it is haunting that the Passerine "gives a call not heard/ at any other time/ beginning with a single, begging note" and leaves the speaker "songless at his far-carrying/ flight song".

Interested as the collection is in oratory, a number of poems in *Had I a Thousand Lives* reflect on the erosion of language. These include "Forcing Music to Speak", "A Religion of Writing", and "Asking for the Alphabet Back", which recalls Heaney's "Alphabets" and Brian Friel's *Translations* in mourning the loss of the Irish language "as English followed the roads, its tidings'/ malady amputating the wildscape". A fascinating poem, "The Mirror Game", remembers Leonardo da Vinci's mirror writing and his statement: "The voice does not work without time". Reminiscent of Heaney's poem "Widgeon" (dedicated to Paul Muldoon), McGuckian sets the corporeality of the poetic voice against the mutability of time to explore silence or the possibility of there being no voice as in "the moment just before you make the sound".

Amid the lyrical musings of poems, and notwithstanding McGuckian's tendency to leave metaphors drowsily swimming around, there is a sharper poetic voice emerging here, as in "The Chimney Boys", whose terse tercets offer a brief nod towards Blake. This polemical voice emerges again in "The Gregory Quarter-acre Clause" and "Filming the Famine" where McGuckian refers to recent films made about the Potato Famine and compares Irish suffering with that of the European Jews from "Crystal Night". This is less an elision of specific historical circumstances and more an exploration of the human cost of oppression. "Jeszcze Polska", the title of which remembers the rallying cry "Poland has not yet perished", is dedicated to Dawid Sierakowiak who chronicled his last days starving in the Lodz Ghetto. Here, as in other poems from the collection, the poet longs for spiritual strength amid historical carnage. The strength of *Had I a Thousand Lives* is found in McGuckian's belief that song or the poetic voice, however fragile and mutable, is her best available answer to "all these injured things".

SARAH FULFORD

A sense of wonder

Jennifer Moxley, *Imagination Verses*, £8.95, Salt, ISBN 1876857943
The Sense Record, £8.95, Salt, ISBN 1876857935

Jennifer Moxley's central concern in *Imagination Verses* is the attempt to make sense of the relation between the self and its surroundings, a concern explored repeatedly through a number of different voices. There are recurrent allusions to alternative historical or mythological selves, direct ventriloquisms of Romantic poets, and more allusive mediations, as in "Aeolian Harp" in *The Sense Record*. Here Coleridge's simile has become a metaphor; the harp appears in the title alone, and it is the addressee John Wilkinson whose "ribboning dreams unspool" and who himself becomes the instrument as he is called upon to "remember when / you thought yourself less played upon by circumstance". Yet such presences gain significance primarily from their association with the lyric "I". In "Little Brick Walk" the old bearded man has no message to impart other than that which the writer imputes to him. In "The Second Winter" a departing lover simultaneously imagines herself as Venus in "the fluted shell of my origin", and reflects self-consciously on the process by which she constructs the likeness:

> In dejection I leave for the island
> of Lutecia. Selfish traveller
> should I, I wonder, record the fatigue?
> Opening lines aside …
> [. . .]
> as on wet sand a tidal film of salt
> in shimmer archives the departing wave
> so will translucence from these pages
> form in vacuous presence an echo
> delightful for a shorter span of time
> than metamorphoses, which move off trace
> unto design, replacing silhouettes
> with more enduring forms of loveliness.

The crabbed syntax, the inversions, and the half-rhymes which seem to parody the very idea of literary language are characteristic of Moxley; it seems that "poetry" is itself one of the experiences or constraints to be mediated. Sometimes the effect is startling, as in the repetitions in "Impervious to Starlight", another poem from *The Sense Record*:

> we saw a long corridor of haunted lawn
> possessed of a vessel atop a pedestal
> of the most exquisite pocked gray marble
> (but wait, *there's more*) we saw a *long* corridor,
> of *haunted* lawn, there was a vessel
> of pocked *marble* atop a *pedestal*

In this instance the added emphases combine paradoxically with the overtly archaic diction in an urgent attempt to make it new, questioning what it is about this language that is shared. Yet the lines also point to a further characteristic of Moxley's: an odd lack of distinction between the record of the senses and that of imagination. Despite the contrast between the titles of these two companion collections, both sense and imagination are ultimately centred on the observing "I" in its various manifestations. In "Impervious to Starlight", the senses are imagined; conversely, in one of the first of the *Imagination Verses*, the action of the imagination is represented in physical form: "This / house is a small space of rearrangements, / a paint box for important revolutions . . . . This house has given us objects to search for / with the comfort that they do exist." It seems that the blurring of boundaries is deliberate – designed to emphasize the lyric freedom to think feelings and feel thoughts. Moxley's poems have previously been described as dream narratives, and at best they have the unsettling quality of dream, of something significant conveyed in time-worn forms. At other times, however, the self threatens to become something of an albatross. In "The Best American Poetry", Moxley writes with confidence that "Nothing matters that is not made to matter" – but she sometimes concentrates so hard on making things matter that the matter itself is lost, as in the title poem of *The Sense Record* :

> I suppose that I have half-imagined
> my remembrances to be fissures
> through which this place makes known
> the continuance of my absent friends,
> as stars sometime were thought the holes
> through which angelic light came shining.

This is momentarily breath-taking, yet even while it assigns the self a negative capability, it says nothing of the friends themselves except that they exist in the mind. Despite a large number of named and unnamed dedicatees and addressees, and despite the delicate and affectionate "Three Graces", in which three male friends are allusively captured, both Moxley's books are strikingly depopulated. Even the self may be other than human; in *The Sense*

Record it is several times figured as a bird, alive and reckless as in "The Best American Poetry", but more often dead, as in "The Lock", "Soleil Cou Coupe", and "Fixed Idea". In the first three poems, the equation is implicit, the lightest possible of touches. In "Fixed Idea", by contrast, even the title seems to mock both the recurrence of the image and the way in which the poem makes the dead bird merely an excuse for an exercise in sensibility; it is not, in the end, "made to matter", except as an occasion for soliloquy. Such self-awareness is integral to Moxley's writing. What in "Impervious to Starlight" is a serious concern – the need mentally to enact "the miracles of daily maintenance" – is satirized in Prufrockian style in the penultimate part of "The Sense Record":

> Life keeps insisting. Nights I worry
> about the spiders inside the vacuum cleaner.
> I notice the squirrels look simian bounding,
> foot over branch, about the trees
> and I wonder if I wasted my youth
> imagining this future.

Moxley has a disarming awareness of the dangers of her own method of writing. It is not necessarily a valid criticism to say that each of these books is ultimately a record of the imagination rather than the senses. Like the earlier Romantics, Moxley dons her mantle consciously and intelligently, and this is precisely the kind of paradox that she delights in.

JANE GRIFFITHS

When the camel's knees fold

Fanny Howe, *Gone*, University of California Press, $16.95, ISBN 0520238109
Richard Greenfield, *A Carnage in the Lovetrees*, University of California Press, $16.95, ISBN 0520238095

New California Poetry, the University of California Press poetry series edited by the poets Robert Hass, Calvin Bedient, and Brenda Hillman, has now published eleven books. Fanny Howe's *Gone* (her second book in the series) and Richard Greenfield's *A Carnage in the Lovetrees* have little in common beyond the press's signature high-quality design and production. Howe is increasingly recognised, thanks in part to the series, as a pre-eminent American poet. Greenfield is a doctoral candidate in Creative Writing at the University of Denver. His is a first book.

For over thirty-five years Fanny Howe published a shelf of books, poetry, and fiction, with small and smaller presses in America and the United Kingdom. This gained her the position Louis Zukofsky named "barely and widely": barely known but widely published. Her *Selected Poems*, published two years ago by the University of California Press and distributed nationally, changed this status. She now reads and teaches across America, and critics and young poets are discovering her work.

The poet Howe most resembles is Emily Dickinson. Like Dickinson's, Howe's poetry is a spiritual diary. She, too, is a metaphysical poet whose subjects are love, death, heaven, hell, eternity, and language. Like Dickinson, Howe is at the heart of her poems; she is intimate but rarely personal. She is an American individualist seeking, at times despairingly, to lose herself in the greater glory of her God. She has gone far from home, but, again like Dickinson, she is a New Englander to the bone.

This resemblance extends to the poets' methods. Dickinson wrote constantly and bound her poems in small booklets she stored or hid in a desk drawer. Howe has described throwing her poems over her shoulder until a drift accumulates and/or a publisher comes along to sweep up behind her. While Howe's language is not exalted like Dickinson's, both poets share a certain anonymity, a quality of timelessness. Howe almost never uses proper names; her "he" and "she" are everyman and everywoman. Her language is spare, and if you found a signature from *Gone* on the street you might not be able to tell exactly when or where in the last fifty years the poems had been written. Like the nineteenth-century Dickinson who found her readers and contemporaries in the twentieth-century, Howe will find her contemporaries in the future.

Gone is divided into five titled sections; the shortest, "Shadows", is three pages long and the longest, "The Passion", is seventy. Except for "Doubt", a prose meditation on Virginia Woolf, Edith Stein, and Simone Weil, and their attempts to find "salvation in a choice in words", the sections are related to, but different from, the serial poem. No single poem can communicate the sequences' ongoingness and rush, the way that the individual poems accumulate associations and impact. But the tang of her voice is in every poem. Here is a short one that, like the majority, is untitled:

> Leave him hanging
> Never call
> His coat is open
> His belt will fall
> These are the actions
> In hospital, woman or jail
>
> When the camel's knees fold
> It is the end of poetry

Howe is half-Irish, Irish enough to see in a man's falling pants the harsh comedy of illness, sex and crime. This is Beckett country. Her final couplet has the virtue of quotability. Howe seems certain to ride that camel to exhaustion.

If you cannot find Howe's *Selected Poems*, *Gone* is a good place to enter her work. Her poetry has less changed over time than evolved, filled out, and grown into itself. In *Gone* she is at the top of her considerable powers.

Graham Greene remarked that childhood is the writer's first capital. In *A Carnage in the Lovetrees*, Richard Greenfield spends his, piecemeal. The emotional core of his book is childhood, his family, and the unexpected death of a sister. Greenfield favours an indirect attack and presents his material so as to avoid journalistic facts and verisimilitude. Perhaps the bigger subject of his book is his attempt to write the sort of poem he needs to write.

In her blurb, the poet Cole Swenson has it exactly in describing Greenfield's poems as "building slowly from pieces scattered, even shattered". It is not surprising that Greenfield is a collagist. This is one tool which Pound and Eliot left us for communicating simultaneity of emotions and anxiety – Greenfield's generation uses the word stress – in the modern world. Greenfield fuses his scattered pieces into prose paragraphs, some as short as sentences: "He awoke in the tent of thunder./ He couldn't see a thing in there except for the glow of a wristwatch. / Was he camped on the border between? Forget it." But he prefers a denser paragraph, a sort of everywhichway prose poem, in which each clause of his sentences thrusts nervously forward. Greenfield's talent is as obvious as his youthful incoherence.

The artist's struggle to find out for himself what he requires to commit his art has a long history in America. In this first book Greenfield has discovered what he can do. From here on he may want to smash things up a little. His poems sound the same, which is the sort of accomplishment that must be gone beyond. Certainly he will want to learn how to vary his rhythms for emotional effect. When he does break his signature surge, as in this passage from "Elegy for the Swing", the effect is piercing:

> Style is all.
> My gone-is-she-gone-
> She is.

Most American arts organizations, publishers included, have a policy of supporting "emerging" artists. Unfortunately, the idea that only the young emerge rules. New California Poetry deserves a salute for acting on the notion that a poet can emerge at any time in her career. By all means support the new and fresh like Richard Greenfield but in poetry, at least, what is new is not, as Fanny Howe's work demonstrates, synonymous with youth.

WILLIAM CORBETT

That contemporary tone of voice

Philip Gross, *Mappa Mundi*,
Bloodaxe, £7.95, ISBN 1852246227

This book is a map of the world as seen from the perspective of amiable – and firmly married – middle age (the word "we" is used throughout with deliberate relish). While the author documents a number of excursions abroad, including to Canada and to Israel, the emphasis is firmly on the cosily English domestic, the world of coupledom and parental responsibility. The somewhat sleepy opening poem sets the tone:

> … it's six in the morning
> and no one at home. The world
> appears, all its things in it,
> imprinting your sight with its skyline.

Mappa Mundi has a number of clear strengths. As well as a good ear, Gross is blessed with a vivid – and quite cinematic – imagination, a source of numerous sharp images: "the puddle-glassed librarian", "a rainbow stump", "the back wall of a gutted petrol station, its price-sign still swinging". This talent finds apt and frequent use in the recreation of dream-situations, often deployed as counterweights to humdrum homeliness. In "Like Knives", for instance, he imagines lovemaking in an environment threateningly full of sharp mechanical objects (one thinks of *Crash*) and the effect is at once suggestive and sinister:

> . . . a probe of moonlight
> on the single bedroll, on us
> at it like knives
> between the nitrous oxide cylinders,
> the castor feet of iron sided cots
>
> not built for babies . . .

In an age when politicians don't want to sound like politicians (Blair) and businessmen don't want to sound like businessmen (Branson), it shouldn't be too surprising that poets often don't want to sound like poets. In *Mappa Mundi* that contemporary tone of voice, what might be called the Ingratiating Idiomatic, is noticeably prevalent – to the book's disadvantage. Gross, in default mode, can sound like Simon Armitage at second-hand:

> I can't blame the barber, what with it
> being dingy four p.m., what with his life
>
> being difficult, as he told me, as he'd told
> the back-and-sides before . . .

Rather in the way that Dolby stereo creates the impression of a movie taking place all around the spectator, the accumulated devices in *Mappa Mundi* tend to work towards closing the book's distance from the reader, or at least (as with Blair and Branson) *appearing* to. Gross likes, for instance, to take his reader by the elbow while pointing things out: "But/ see, it takes their weight"; "See the crack in the door/ with the moon looking in?"; "See the single holes / where the eggs were drilled in". To sound conversational he uses a lot of italics: ("Sea? No, the *ocean*?" "finding *everything* there/ for the taking" "going shy and headlong towards something vaguely *more*"). A more frequent strategy which aims for immediacy, is to give the impression of poems being formed at the same time as the actions which they describe, or at the same time as the poems are transmitted ("OK / you know there's nothing / really blue up there"; "Yes, there were witnesses" "No, // let's drift to the dining-room"). In similar vein, he is fond of the drama of self-correction, for example via negative exclamation ("You're / flying, no, being // flown" "a radar dish, no, five or six / of them" "a genteel caravan/ knee-deep in the Channel, no, a carriage // bogged down in a ford") and theatrically wavering definition ("like how she lifts a – what you can't / make out" "the kind of voices just not right for – what, as I opened my eyes" "coming out of the forest with / is that a unicorn?").

Initially, such effects are colourful, and I imagine they would work well enough in a one-off performance situation. Read more than once, however, they pale; the book comes to seem mechanical – "effectful" rather than effective. Some of these tricks remind one of soap opera dialogue, artificially generating dramatic interest of the "It's-a-nice-day-out-Bill-oh-no-it-isn't-Ben" variety. Occasionally, the verbalisms barely mask a bathetic vagueness: "Something like a token / of obscure esteem"; "a kind of pyramid, a kind of tomb"; "We'd left / something behind – something and also the sense of why // that thing had mattered". It made me think of *Exercises in Style*, where Raymond Queneau takes a deliberately trivial incident, a man bumping into another on a bus, and renders it in such a barrage of different modes that the subject, exhilaratingly, becomes style. Gross, on the other hand, takes incidents which are more than banal but less than compelling and treats them with effects which are more than ordinary but less than outstanding. He doesn't go far enough in the direction either of lively style or of lively content and the result is a pleasant but patchy book.

JOHN REDMOND

Aiming for a near miss

Anthony Howell, *Dancers in Daylight*,
Anvil Press, £9.95, ISBN 0856463647

Poetic form, as Auden reminds us, "frees us from the fetters of self". In his seventh collection, the poet and dancer Anthony Howell proves the wisdom of these words. Always adept at word-play and delighting in the natural world, Howell's poetry can be funny and, at times, touching. Too often, though, one sees the benefits form brings through its absence in this book; and, where Howell does employ form, its effect is sometimes mixed.

The collection divides into five sections, made up of longer narrative poems such as the title poem, "Border Country", or "The Holiday", and short poems about the poet's life, such as "Macalpine", "Hermitage", or "Nil By Mouth". The longer poems are written in (sometimes very) rough pentameters, whereas the shorter poems make more use of rhymes and formal metres. Unfortunately, there is not much evidence of any form, or lack thereof, being used to suit the purpose of a poem – one reason, perhaps, why the collection contains few complete successes and some poems which read as being either half-finished, or candidates for exclusion.

When Howell's poetry does work, the effect can be powerful, as in "1944", "Lost Children", "Cathar Country", or "From Queribus". In these poems Howell relies on more than incident written out in verse, or a sense of humour, to carry his meaning. It is clear that he has something to say in each of these pieces that merits subtle treatment – as when he writes about the survivors of the Nazi holocaust in "1944":

> it was usual to scratch
> the last of your lice
> and rock on your haunches
> calmly watching the bulldozers
> pushing matchsticks into a trench.

Again in "Lost Children", concerns about form disappear thanks to Howell's assured rhythm and controlled diction; as when, for instance, he is imagining the "odd one, the simply forgotten / Missing, but not missed… / Trawling for bottles on deserted beaches".

The title poem, "Dancers in Daylight", is a more qualified success. Here Howell mixes scenes from the Greek myths with his own fantasies to explore the nature of sexual desire, and in doing so gives the pleasing impression of having controlled his voice:

> with ingles there
> to clamber up to, laughingly lie down in,
> lovingly to kiss the languid skin
> of some enchanting shoulder.

These successes aside, there will inevitably be lesser poems in a collection that exceeds the length of the entire mature output in verse of Larkin or Dylan Thomas. This book might have benefited from the exclusion of poems such as "Grimus Merdae", with its cheap rhymes and tired puns, or "Two Portraits: Son". In this poem, the over-use of a single rhyme turns self-description into a weird, postmodern Krishna mantra: "he who pops / pills and slops his coffee…and crops / his thinning hair too seldom…and props / Himself awake, considering full stops?"

Most interesting are the almost failures, the not-quite-there poems that make up half or more of *Dancers in Daylight*. At the end of "Interruptions" Howell notes that, "A near miss is what I've been / Aiming for, baby, most of my life", and on the evidence of much of this book, he has succeeded. In places, promising ideas are spoiled by the use of cliché ("Shrivelled like a prune"), by grating internal rhymes ("she unzips and grips her dress"), or over-wrought word play: "the campus ramps rumpus gathers speed". Elsewhere, the temptation to reach for an easy conclusion capped with an end-stopped full rhyme is one Howell finds hard to resist: "I'll be darned if I find one on mine / But that's fine. That's fine."

For all of these criticisms, it would be wrong to deny Howell's quirky humour, and his talent for observation, especially his eye for natural detail. In some of the better poems, Howell puts human feelings in their place by setting them against the greater canvas of nature, as in "Border Country". But our appreciation of this kind of delicacy is compromised elsewhere by the Kipling-style mimicry of cockney accents and the somewhat high-handed treatment of London's poor, as in "Memories of The Old Days in Adamstown". Such moments show the less desirable side of Howell's gentlemanly and romantic sensibility.

JAMES W. WOOD

Red letter daze

Sean Bonney, *Poisons, their antidotes*,
West House Books, £5, ISBN 1904052142

T he cover of Sean Bonney's new book is by fellow-poet Jeff Hilson. Title
and author's name emerge from a clutter of distressed lettering. Lines
of smaller type run across vertically, making what looks like an arrow:
a rune scratched on a stone long ago. Now desktop software makes typo-
graphical perfection commonplace, designers often catch the eye with worn
and broken type: what's unusual here is that lettrist sabotage is not restricted
to the cover, but signals an armoury of effects inside the book.

Sean Bonney is celebrated on the London poetry scene for startling
performances, edgy and rhythmic, charged with a political fury few poets
muster. An anarchist from Manchester, he was drawn to poetry by attending
the late Bob Cobbing's Writers Forum workshops. Cobbing declared that
anything on a page could be "performed", and proved his case by reciting
poems which consisted of a single giant letter, bizarre scrambles of print,
marks and shadows, or photocopied litter. As might be expected, Cobbing's
antics went down better with music fans than with readers. However, his
attention to the coordinates of sign, sound and meaning were far from
random, and became a rallying point for poets who believe poetry should
unleash the immanent music of language. Focusing on the brute materials of
ink, paper and vocal sound, Writers Forum turned their back on mass-media
"communication": their reputation as "avant garde" spelt inaccessibility to the
majority.

Sean Bonney is a little different. Coming from a political generation who
saw Thatcher's regime wrecked by the Poll Tax Riot in Trafalgar Square in
1991, and then the World Trade Organisation transformed into an
international pariah by the Battle of Seattle in 1999, Bonney doesn't suffer
from the social alienation which caused many '60s wordsmiths to retreat into
personal universes, brilliant but blind. Bonney's affection for the populism of
the Beats is evident. Although a cursory glance at *Poisons, their antidotes* might
have some muttering "free verse" and returning the volume to the shelf, there
is a rationale behind his eccentric typography. These poems are scores for
impassioned recitation, burning with a rare urgency and intelligence.

The opening piece uses overprinting to evoke the stutter of someone
overcome by the emotional effect of what they're describing. Written before
London news items about seagulls building nests in high-rise blocks ("cliffs")
and attacking passers-by ("egg-raiders"), the poem's oracular obsession with

the bird/word rhyme is alarming: Hitchcock in typeset. Two longish poems document walks in central London. There are no typographical experiments here. They have a raw quality: manic states transcribed in phrases short enough to catch them. Because the poems are written for Bonney's speaking voice, they have an elegant rhythmic flow: this elegance provides a foil for the desperation and violence of the content. Drinking coffee and thinking about the attack on Iraq, walking in Soho and thinking about Paul Verlaine and the Paris Commune, Bonney makes historic events part of his existence.

At the climax of the volume are four poems which use overlaid type in the manner of Hilson's cover. Visually, they're like symbols witnessed in a dream, opaque to interpretation yet utterly determinate (when Hollywood decided to portray dreams as blurry and out of focus, it made a fundamental error). At first, I saw the shapes as drinks lined up in front of an alcoholic (a Guinness, cocktails with ice and straw, etc): addictive consumption shorn of the frivolity and evasion of advertising. Moving the eye from one to another, the shapes shift and extend, invoking alchemy, sex magick and the poet's desperate impulse to communicate personal excitements with manipulating the verbal stuff. Nothing quite so hair-raising – nothing illustrating quite so clearly the capacity of a small book to intimate a new set of connections, affiliations and desires – has arrived since Iain Sinclair's *Lud Heat* in 1975.

Bonney's debut *Notes on Heresy* (Writers Forum, 2002) was strong, but there the verse hadn't totally absorbed the political argument. *Poisons, their antidotes* is an auspicious development because, even though he adheres to the phrasing of his speaking voice, Bonney has not trapped himself in a manner. The literary historian will discern skillful deployment of forms associated with such writers as Tom Raworth, Maggie O'Sullivan and Allen Fisher – nevertheless, no grounding in these writers is needed to feel the heat of Bonney's expression, something born out by the many "non-poetry" friends I've lent the book to. One hopes that lovers of poems written in gentler modes won't reject such intensity simply because it's too hot for a ho-hum reaction.

BEN WATSON

My, how they've grown

Helen Vendler, *Coming of Age as a Poet,*
Harvard University Press, $22.95, ISBN 0674010248

Helen Vendler has the right idea about poems: that they are structures of felt thought which may be more thoroughly appreciated through attentive reading. But she has the wrong idea about poets: that they are a separate species.

The phenomenon anthropologised by the metaphor of her title is an interesting one. In an advanced literary (as opposed to an oral) culture, poets distinguish themselves by the individuality of their style and subject matter. For the most serious, this amounts to a private aesthetic and ethical project: to tune language to a world-view. The detailed demonstration of how this is achieved is one of the most interesting products of literary research.

Coming of Age does not contain significant new research; rather, it gives a set of close-readings contextualised by reference to published juvenilia and later work. By "Coming of Age", Vendler means specifically the moment in a poet's ouevre when he or she produces – pop, like an egg – his or her first "perfect" poem. Originally a series of lectures, the book awards the school prize in turn to: Milton ("L'Allegro"); Keats ("On First Looking into Chapman's Homer"); Eliot ("The Love Song of J. Alfred Prufrock"); and Plath ("The Colossus").

As an internationally-respected close-reader, it was perhaps inevitable that Vendler should choose to build her case around single poems. The idea is appealingly neat. With this "perfect" poem, the Young Poet became the Great Poet. By "perfect", Vendler means "confidence, mastery, and above all, ease. . . they manifest a coherent and well-managed idiosyncratic style voiced in memorable lines; one would not wish them other than they are". "Well-managed"; "memorable"; "one would not wish…" The definition is not watertight. Inevitably, the application of "perfect" as a literary historical label will depend on the taste and temperament of the critic.

A solemn but erroneous assumption informs Vendler's choices. Being a young poet is "painful" and "heroic". "The thrashing about that young poets do. . . is often both comic and painful to observe, and even more painful, of course, to endure." To write a successful poem is an "ultimately heroic effort".

Though it may be painstaking, writing, for a writer, is not painful. The Young Poet is a self-anointed creature, practising something which gives pleasure. W.H. Auden described the experience more accurately as one that actually alleviates the miseries of growing up: "Lying awake at night in your single bed you are conscious of a power by which you will survive the wallpaper of your boarding house or the expensive bourgeois horrors of your home" (*The Sea and the Mirror*).

Implicitly, Vendler's assumption leads to another: that the young writer's "pain" is only fully relieved by properly serious outbursts. So, in the chapter on Keats ("Perfecting the Sonnet"), we are asked to consider "On First Looking Into Chapman's Homer" and "On Sitting Down to Read King Lear Once Again". Vendler's essay concludes:

> Another young poet might have remained content with the "perfect" sonnet on Homer. Keats's depth of heart and mind required that he go on to enter, within a year, the burning nest of the Phoenix to write the sonnet of Shakespearean fruit, and forest, and fire.

In other words, having written one good sonnet, Keats, "within a year" (brave man), wrote another, with a different rhyme scheme. Why Vendler considers this a remarkable feat of persistence is not clear: does she assume that "another young poet" would have framed his 14 lines, put them on the mantelpiece, and taken up skittles? The critical narrative is romanticised. Keats, a week before the Lear sonnet, produced another exquisitely observed, variant Petrarchan sonnet. But – presumably because it was addressed "To Mrs. Reynold's Cat" – Vendler doesn't mention it.

In the case of T. S. Eliot, this romantic selectivity chooses "Prufrock" over "Portrait of a Lady". Although the iconic "Prufrock" is undoubtedly the *more* memorable of the two, Eliot's early talent cannot be considered immature when it produces the bathetic, musical, painful and cruel "Portrait" (to return to the definition of "perfect": "a coherent and well-managed idiosyncratic style voiced in memorable lines"). It is telling that, in this chapter's final paragraph, Vendler's summary of Eliot's later development goes straight from "Prufrock" to *The Waste Land*. Indeed, in her previous book – *Seamus Heaney* – Vendler, paraphrasing wildly, completely confused the two: "a screen on which one can read the patterns of the nerves on a given day (as Eliot justly said in *The Waste Land*)". Skipping the "Other Observations" of Eliot's first book, and the difficult, crystalline *Poems 1920*, betrays a critical temperament more interested in intellectual melodrama than subtle and exacting writing.

That said, in her final and most persuasive chapter, Vendler mounts a welcome and intelligent defence of Sylvia Plath against the charge of melodramatic self-absorption. "The demand that a writer have not merely a vision but a 'positive' vision seems to me unjust", she writes, rightly, going on to praise Plath instead for her dogged opposition to "niceness".

Vendler does a professional job of sorting out the swag-bag of influences which Plath hungrily jumbled together in her juvenilia, returning each tone to its owner: Lowell, Frost, Yeats. She then argues irrefutably that, after discovering her uniquely cool and "impertinent" poetic manner in "The Colossus", Plath worked hard towards greater human inclusiveness (the example given is "Parliament Hill Fields").

Unfortunately, although the close-readings are patient and mostly logical, Vendler fails to notice some important things about lines which she herself singles out. When, for example, in "The Colossus", Plath talks of "Counting the red stars and those of plum-color", Vendler explains, unilluminatingly, "She numbers the stars and relishes their different colors". But surely the sing-song circumlocution, "those of plum-color", goes deeper, bringing obliquely to our attention how detached the speaker feels (as so often in Plath) from the life-colours, the bright and the dark blood-reds.

Similarly, in "Parliament Hill Fields", an elegy for Plath's miscarried child, Vendler tells us that the line "Already your doll grip lets go" is a "keystone". But she doesn't explain why. My explanation would be that the image is touchingly, conflictingly active and passive: it suggests that the emotionally-confused speaker resembles the child she doesn't have, blaming dolly for being dropped. We are obliquely prepared for this complicated and condensed self-analysis by the digressive observation in the previous stanza of a schoolgirl dropping a "barrette of pink plastic". Vendler, however, misses the connection and criticises the digression: "The detail… may be intended as a parallel to the 'inconspicuous' lost fetus, but if so, the image is too remote and inanimate to strike home". Judiciously resisting the crude metaphorical explanation, she misses the subtle one.

Coming of Age as a Poet is a pertinent cross-period critical investigation imperfectly conducted. Vendler has a fondness for scientific-looking precision: an appendix listing and classifying all of Keats's sonnets by rhyme scheme ("To Mrs. Reynold's Cat" is a "P2a"); a sentence by Milton "graphed" into stepped sections (so that it looks like William Carlos Williams in a ruff). Her underlying attitude to her subjects, however, is romantically selective. And the close readings on which the book rests its case are sometimes just that: close, but no cigar.

JEREMY NOEL-TOD

Poetry Chronicle

John Temple, *Collected Poems*, Salt, £9.95, ISBN 1876857560; Vahni Capildeo
No Traveller Returns, Salt, £9.95, ISBN 1876857889; Anne Blonstein,
the blue pearl, Salt, £8.95, ISBN 187685765X; M.T.C. Cronin,
beautiful, unfinished PARABLE /SONG/CANTO/POEM, Salt, £8.95,
ISBN 1876857293; Ethan Paquin, *Accumulus*, Salt, £8.95, ISBN 1844710157;
Jaime Saenz, *Immanent Visitor* , University of California Press, £12.95,
ISBN 0520230485; Maggie O'Sullivan, *Palace of Reptiles*,
The Gig Press (Nate Dorward, 109 Hounslow Ave, Willowdale, ON, M2N
2B1, Canada: ndorward@sprint.ca), £8 (incl.p&p); Gabriel Gudding,
A Defense of Poetry, University of Pittsburgh Press, $12.95, ISBN 0822957868

Salt, the Cambridge-based independent publisher, is emerging as a
significant force in the literary marketplace. Unencumbered, it would
appear, by any dogmatic vision of "their" kind of poetry, and
maintaining a spring-tide high output, this is an encouraging and altogether
commendable enterprise. Whatever cavils come hereafter, they should be kept
firmly in the context of whole-hearted appreciation that these books exist at
all.

John Temple's *Collected Poems* gathers together thirty-five years of pre-
dominantly lyrical works. By deft use of collage, quotation and spatial
recasting, a distinctive voice is gleaned from the ephemera of everyday
language. Songs, sound-bites and occasional reading are transformed by a
subtle insistence on their other, half-hidden meanings. Temple is, by turns,
wittily political, deploying epigrammatic arrow-shafts, and full of pathos. In,
for example, "An Evening Walk", a Tom Jones song is intercut with descrip-
tions, and clever enjambment splits single words over the line-end to give sly
ironic alternatives. Thus "the song ex / pressed in the young / man's shoulders"
concatenates pressure and expression: by fissuring the "ex" from "pressed"
Temple allows it to suggest the "ex"-partner in the song. Vahni Capildeo's first
collection, *No Traveller Returns*, weighs in only eight pages shy of Temple's
Collected; and although it provides ample evidence of a poet of some ability,
such a door-stopping début seems to suggest a slightly timid approach to self-
selection. Although Capildeo can write with immense and satisfying
precision, there are also moments where a profusion of adjectives and
subclauses stymies the strength of the image. That said, the mammoth central
section, "The Monster Scrapbook", is a fierce, funny and genuinely

imaginative take on ideas of identity and difference, dependence and exclusion.

Anne Blonstein, like John Temple, is skilful in the deploying of other texts within the poetry of *the blue pearl*. Whereas in Temple's work the fragments are synthesised into a new voice, Blonstein – whose major theme throughout the collection is the relationship between shard and artefact, actual gap and imagined completeness – these borrowed elements remain discrete. What does bind them together is a sculptural sense of placing on the page; and, although at times it can make the work seem rather obviously structured, at its best it creates a vibrant tessellation, wholly fitting the content to the form.

On the other hand, M.T.C. Cronin's *beautiful, unfinished PARABLE /SONG/CANTO/POEM*, despite some elegance of construction and attention to detail, seems never quite to gel into anything more memorable. "You cannot speak to one person / with words meant / for many people", she writes, and yet the language remains resolutely quotidian. Lines like

> The nicest thing
> about children
> is that they do not know
>
> They are timeless

seem more akin to the "inspiring" words on an Athena poster than contemporary poetry. Such sentimentalities crop up continually, syrupy jolts that overpower the subtler and more substantial flavours of the work.

All four of these titles have the capacity to earn, and reward, their own readership. The fifth title from Salt, Ethan Paquin's *Accumulus*, is in a different league altogether: a book that is both necessary and genuinely inspiring. For anyone at all concerned with the craft, challenges and scope for meaning in modern poetics, Ethan Paquin is a must-read.

The antecedent condition for Paquin's aesthetic vision is outlined in the poem "Like an Empty: *after Chuang Tzu*". The poet meditates on the nameless "black center / of the flower" and the nameless "condition of identifying with a rock / plashed with a river all day" in contrast to his own possession of a name. It ends:

> Imagine what the petals or the river would
> think of this lack of human priority
>
> (a condition, incidentally, also nameless)

What Paquin's poetry does is constantly to assail the as-yet-anonymous experience in a torrent of vocabulary, neologism, metaphor, and collocation. This is poetry which requires to be read with a dictionary alongside and an alert mind; not because Paquin is indulging in the recondite or vaunting some superior grasp of language, but because he has a genuine desire for exactness. Grackle, molassia, awrap, sentencery: the poems are coaxed out of their plight of silence by such gloriously specific and creative terms.

Paquin guides the reader with a beautiful passage capturing the method of reading:

> There is some whirligig word en aspera
> and I've almost caught the elusive thing but it gurgles –
> pretty much a protest, elegant and hurt dazzling.

Language – pyrotechnical, giddying, replete as it is – is nonetheless the means not the end of *Accumulus*. Paquin outlines his major themes with clarity: in "Apostasy", he balances the "revelation of a fraudulent life, / yes, a sad but not / entirely unexpected moment …" with the "healing / in the uncontrollable / beauty of not this world". His world is one where God is either "lonely" or "has given up", where love can never entirely satisfy desire, and where "pornographers made us look at trees differently". It is in this context that the language assumes its vital importance: everything is hard-won, and nothing is taken on trust. Complexity is a moral choice. "I've long taken humanity in measured little doses, a blizzard of it now I'll welcome" states the narrator of "Diary": a possible redemption is in "scavenging the fine print". This collection contains material previously issued by Stride publications in *The Makeshift*. Salt are doing excellent work, and they are not alone.

The University of California Press's bilingual edition of the *Selected Poems* of Jaime Saenz (*Immanent Visitor*, translated by Kent Johnson and Forrest Gander) is a welcome redress to the dearth of Latin American poetry available to the English reader. The Bolivian poet Saenz (1921–1986) was an almost archetypal late Romantic: politically, sexually and aesthetically an outsider, and an alcoholic to boot.

His poetry, at first sight, can appear meandering, its long lines unspooling across the page. It is, however, worth persisting with. The "listlessness" is actually densely structured, with clauses that deliberately qualify, contradict or invert what goes before. The result is, in fact, not torpid at all; but energetic with its own chronic uncertainty: "In a word: there is and is not communication; and you don't exist, and I cease to exist in concerning myself with you, since I leave myself so that you may exist", he writes, explaining, in the next line, "– in conclusion, I'm telling you that this is the tone to use to penetrate matters of love – a dark thing / / for whose explanation the tone will need to

be dark." The paradoxes of Saenz's poetry are present because his favourite topics – the you and I of love, the I and not-I of death – are inherently paradoxical. As in the next two books, the poet embeds in the poetry the key to unlocking it.

Maggie O'Sullivan's *Palace of Reptiles* can be a disorientating place for the casual browser. Incantatory, hallucinatory, like an idea of choreography but without the physical presence in which to ground the movements, this is clearly recognisable as avant-garde work. "It's easy to loss here", as she says, in this place of

ASSEMBLAGES, after Kurt Schwitters who made superb
use of the UN- the NON and the LESS – THE UNREGARDED,
the found, the cast-offs, the dismembered materials.

Like Shakespeare's Autolycus, the "snapper-up of unconsidered trifles", O'Sullivan constructs a shifting montage out of scraps of *Finnegans Wake*, art-theory, bestiaries, and slogans. To look in it for "a meaning" (as one might say that the meaning of Wilfred Owen's "Dulce et Decorum Est" is "War, what is it good for?") is to miss the point. Each reading *should* generate different meanings, coincidences, and snatches of story. Like a kaleidoscope, it is pointless only if you expect to see the same pattern each time.

Gabriel Gudding's *A Defense of Poetry* won the Agnes Lynch Starrett Prize in 2001. Humour and poetry are often uneasy bedfellows: stand up comedy relies on a "get it at once or not at all" approach and poetry, oppositely, grows with re-reading. Gudding may be a comic poet, but even so the work has a lingering quality. "Adolescence" is a good introduction, a perfectly horrid fable of what hatched out of Humpty-Dumpty.

There is a lot of scatology; good enough for Dunbar, Swift and e e cummings, but still likely to induce nose-wrinkling in capital-p Poetry circles. Gudding's title poem, a hybrid of Biblical phraseology and The Pharsyde's vituperative hip-hop, introduces the irreverence that runs throughout the collection. It has a cumulative effect: by the time the reader reaches "My Buttocks" on p.77, with the epigraph "your buttocks – Wallace Stevens", it's hard not to be charmed by the panache and sheer devilry.

This does not prevent Gudding being a serious poet, and the last poem in the collection achieves something I had thought (until now) was tantamount to impossible: a good, sincere and unflinching poem about September 11. Dedicated to the "civil libertarians" who died that day, it's a phonetic riot riffing on not blaming anyone: "If not Sonny and Cher, then Sony and Che Guevara?"

STUART KELLY

Artists' Notes

This is the second issue of *Poetry Review* in which Fred Mann has curated the art pages. Three pages each have been given to Cathy de Monchaux (including the cover image) and Gillian Wearing, and two pages celebrate the Whitechapel Gallery exhibition "Atlas" by Gerhard Richter.

Gerhard Richter was born in Dresden in 1932 and grew up under the Third Reich and National Socialism. One of the world's most influential contemporary artists, Richter has helped to re-define contemporary painting. The two works displayed here indicate how he selects the images he uses to create his paintings: images ranging from those of close friends and family to media images of contemporary political events. These references are then altered as he transfers them to canvas. Richter sees photography as a way for painting to progress beyond the politically loaded extremes of Realism or Abstract Expressionism.

Gillian Wearing includes three images from her recent exhibition "Album" (at Maureen Paley, Interim Art) which explores portraiture and family history. Wearing has created masks of her family members' faces and bodies using props and prosthetic devices, and attempts to adopt the identity of each family member, and also that of her own younger self. The resulting portraits seek to examine the psychological impact of families on individuals. Shown here are Wearing's self-portraits as her brother, sister and her father. Only on very close inspection can one see Wearing's eyes in each of the bodies she inhabits.

Cathy de Monchaux makes delicate, sensual and sometimes disturbing sculptures. Using brass, leather, velvet, and fur, de Monchaux creates tableaux of a complex subconscious world that evoke and interpret the psychology of dreams and fantasies, symbolism and beauty. Included in this issue are a series of recent wall and floor works which have been made since her inclusion in the Turner prize in 1998. De Monchaux has also recently collaborated with the musicians Martin Ware and Vince Clarke for her recent "At Home" exhibition at Dominic Berning, London.

For the Whitechapel pages thanks are due to Iwona Blaswick and Andrea Tarsia. Gillian Wearing appears courtesy of Maureen Paley/Interim Art with thanks to Maureen Paley and James Lavender. Cathy de Monchaux appears courtesy of Dominic Berning, London. Fred Mann is a director of Rhodes + Mann, London.

Poet in the Gallery

PAUL FARLEY

Philip Guston: Retrospective
24 January – 12 April 2004
Royal Academy of Arts

If there was one thing everyone knew about Philip Guston when I was at art
school, it was the extraordinary about-turn he made towards the end of
the sixties, abandoning years of tasteful, painterly abstraction and lurching
into . . . well, into a big in-your-face figuration the like of which nobody could
have been expecting. It's difficult now fully to register the shock waves his 1970
show at the Marlborough Gallery must have sent out, although the contem-
porary press (it wasn't universally panned, though everyone remembers the
bad ones: a *New York Times* leader called Guston "A Mandarin pretending to
be a Stumblebum") and reports from on the ground (an embarrassed silence,
according to one person at the private view) suggest the discomfort these new
works must have caused: hooded characters cruising for a bruising in
primitive jalopies (like clapped-out perambulators crossed with sardine tins);
the same cowled and be-sheeted figures chain-smoking their heads off, clock-
watching, painting, and generally scheming under bare bulbs. In a big
retrospective exhibition like this one, it's tempting to look for the signs early
on, the storm clouds gathering perhaps, and to try and nail the exact moment
at which Guston "went electric".

In a curatorial sense the break comes halfway through the show, which
means half of this exhibition contains work from the last ten years of a career
that spanned six decades. From the outset, we're given ample evidence of
recurring themes. Guston had seen the Klan parade in Los Angeles, and had
even seen some paintings he made on this subject slashed by Klansmen. The
first piece here is a drawn study for "Conspirators" from 1930: Klansmen plot
beneath a tree where a black man has been lynched; one carefully inspects a
length of thick rope as if he were a campanologist. After he and his classmate
Jackson Pollock were kicked out of Manual Arts High School in California for
leafleting anti-sports messages, Guston became interested in mural painting,
travelling to Mexico as mural assistant to David Alfaro Siqueiros, and
eventually moving to New York where he fell in with the Federal Arts Project.
He was successful, and secured some good commissions. Around about this
time (the late thirties) there's also a pull towards studio-based work. But in
mural studies such as "Boys Fighting", or in canvases like "The Gladiators" and

"Martial Memory", already we find hoods (paper hats and bags over heads), bin-lids; even in a watercolour and ink study from 1943, his "Parachutes Hung Out to Dry" suggest what was to come, dangling as these do like a Klavern's washing.

After early figuration comes abstraction. A canvas from 1947–8 called "The Tormentors" stands as a watershed, and gradually we lose our grip on recognisable "things" in the world; eventually, even shape breaks down into pure stroke. Cadmium red medium starts to dominate. Guston found himself labelled an "Abstract Impressionist", which I always thought a bit facile, since any resemblances to Monet are superficial. (An essay by Michael Auping in the catalogue makes a much stronger case for the "scaffolding" of Piet Mondrian.) But while Abstract Expressionism, generally (and much is generalised concerning this necessarily disparate bunch) preferred its canvases pretty huge – allowing the viewer to enter or become overwhelmed by the painting's force-field – another essay, by Andrew Graham-Dixon, suggests that the scale of the easel painting "with its implications of an image to be discerned" was never abandoned by Guston, and that the term "Abstract Impressionism" at least implies American-European crossover.

By the end of the fifties, and into the new decade, something is stirring. By 1964's "The Light" and "New Place" (germane titles notwithstanding) the brushstrokes can't help but coalesce around very definite core shapes: shapes that remind us of *things*. And then the fun really begins. There's a hand holding a brush; a shoe; that's definitely a masked head. And between 1968 and 1970, a deluge. Guston said at this time he felt as if he'd taken the lid off something; images stream out. He had a sense of Rembrandt removing the plane of art – "it is not a painting, but a real person – a substitute, a golem" – and paintings like "Edge of Town" or "The Studio" are rendered with such immediacy that you know what he means. A parallel world comes into view, a world whose objects we can recognise but which runs according to its own rules and laws of physics. Those at the Marlborough exhibition got to see this work minus any context-building or lead-ins.

The move into figuration for Guston wasn't accompanied by any lessening of the painterly qualities of these works. If anything, they are heightened. There's this marvellous, direct, assertive application of the paint, and a real sense of the joy of just pushing the stuff around. You get the feeling Guston would have even enjoyed slapping household gloss onto the back of a door; that he must have been as hooked to the feel of a brush as to those cigarettes. He moves easily from buttery, linseed-loaded strokes and daubings to matt turpentine washes, always letting the paint do the talking. Although Piero della Francesca and Rembrandt were the durable twin stars in his firmament, I was reminded of another artist who also achieved an amazing directness in his later work, Titian; another artist who seemed to think and feel in paint.

The old masters of the European tradition loom large over these late paintings – "It thrills me to think of the enormous Past" Guston said – and this represents another break from the tendencies of American painting at that time. While the Abstract Expressionists can be seen as generally conforming to a model of New World frontierism, trailblazing ahead and dispensing with the European past and all its baggage, Guston plugs straight back into that tradition.

Because the show places such an emphasis on Guston's last ten years, there's a chance to tease out more local shifts in style that run counter to this period's routine labelling as "the late work". As a consequence, the work of his final decade becomes even richer and, judging by what's exhibited, can be subdivided into distinct phases: the hooded figures in their salmon-spread-pink landscapes and interiors; the huge heads and all-seeing eyes, rough-shod legs and bin-lid phalanxes that start appearing around the mid-seventies; and the final smaller acrylics with their spidery inks (the scaling-down can be attributed to Guston's failing health about this time: he died of a heart attack, aged sixty-six, in 1980).

When I first saw these late Gustons, I registered their cartoon-like qualities, though I didn't know the half of it. Guston grew up reading "the funnies", and was steeped in popular culture. His expulsion from High School came about partly because of his visual lampoonery: look again at the "San Clemente" paintings and drawings, in which a bollock-faced Richard Nixon drags around a gigantic phlebetic leg. Guston remained a lifelong fan of George Herriman's *Krazy Kat* and Bud Fisher's *Mutt and Jeff*, among many others. I didn't know this work well at all, but was convinced Guston must have known the counterculture comics emerging around the time the first hooded figures appear, especially Robert Crumb's. Not so, according to the catalogue. I was left wondering too about whether the "Kilroy" graffiti had had some influence, especially on canvases like "The Painter", in which a huge smoking head with bloodshot eyes peeks over a Gustonian brick wall. Either way, his appreciation of those funny papers finds some kind of outlet and enlargement in this late work.

These days more people get Guston, but there's still something a bit gristly about him, a bit rough-round-the-edges and difficult to assimilate. When I was looking for a cover for my first collection of poems, I hit upon the idea of using a Guston ladder or light-bulb (because they chimed thematically, and because I was a fan) but this got vetoed by somebody at my publishers, who said the images were "too ugly".

"I got sick and tired of all that purity! Wanted to tell stories." I've carried around that line of Guston's since art college, but what are its implications? That there's a choice to be made between abstraction and figuration? High and low culture? There's a parabola to his career – bolstered by shows like this one, with all its curatorial nudges and "bridging works" – that provides a strong, art-historical narrative. But it seems to me the real choice he made was between fixity and change. Guston was decorated and awarded fellowships early on, but moved away from the work that had brought about that success; he was a well-established, card-carrying member of the biggest art movement in post-war America, but chucked it in again and did what he felt he had to do. This must have been a sacrifice: friends turned their back on him; he parted company with his gallery in 1972, and the new work sold only sluggishly. In one of my favourite paintings here, "The Hand" from 1979, a pinkie-ringed paw holds a cigarette and shows us the time; the sweep hand on the wristwatch is like a white anchor. He'd worked around the clock, and now time was running out. But he got this down. How many other artists since, or writers for that matter, have managed to wreck and re-invent and make a new space for themselves like this one did?

COLLECTION STEDELIJK MUSUEM, AMSTERDAM

Geoffrey Dearmer Prize

We are delighted to announce that the winner of the Geoffrey Dearmer poetry prize 2003 is Rebecca O'Connor, for her poem "A Bag of Tangerines", which was published in *Poetry Review* 92.4 (Summer 2002).

This year's judge was the poet Matthew Welton, who said: "Rebecca O'Connor's 'A Bag of Tangerines' is a poem that occupies itself, and, in that, it does as much as any poem has to. The poem is striking in how simple it appears, but, of course, it can only have this effect because it is put together so well. Like sewing a straight seam or stretching a tight drumskin, making a poem is a matter where the technical achievement is better if it doesn't draw attention to itself. And 'A Bag of Tangerines' is a poem on which the work has definitely been done." Matthew also commended two other shortlisted poems: Jon Woodward's "your eyes are just hanging" (93/2) and Carrie Etter's "Fin de Siècle" (93/2).

Now in its sixth year, the Geoffrey Dearmer Prize was set up with a generous bequest to honour the noted World War One poet, and the Poetry Society's oldest member, Geoffrey Dearmer. By establishing an endowment fund, the Dearmer family have enabled the Poetry Society to award an annual prize to the *Poetry Review* "new poet of the year" who has not yet published a book.

Letters to the Editors

Alastair Campbell

I was appalled to find the likeness of macho bully A. Campbell disfiguring the cover of *Poetry Review*. How is this relevant to poetry?

Those of us who write a poetry of political or social comment do not deliberately set out to expound our beliefs or any particular ideology. We might believe that socialism or feminism, for example, might provide a truer analysis of the world we live in, but these beliefs underlie everything we do, and are therefore integrated into all our activities, including writing poems.

If poetry is about discovering truths in the act of writing, rather than expounding The Truth, or the Party Line, then Campbell is the worst possible model for poets, unless you want to write agitprop and nothing else. Of course writing is never neutral or innocent; it is always informed or conditioned by personal, social or political factors. Yet any real poem should influence our thinking, by telling us things we didn't realise we knew. It should also be an act of discovery for the writer, line by line, without a predetermined outcome.

Poems, especially first person monologues, can of course be fictions, but any poet who believes that lying in public is acceptable should take a job in advertising, or rent themselves to like-minded types in Westminster. Personally, I value poetries informed by socialism or Green politics, but I also value freedom of conscience.

Brian Docherty
London

The Alastair Campbell cover is completely inspired. Everyone I know just howled with laughter when they first saw it. It is like one of those portraits from the Tudor period of Great (paranoid) Men of State. Pure Holbein. The photograph gives the sense of transparency, like the portraits in oils. There Campbell stands, defiant, staring straight at the camera, unflinching – who will blink first? – the great papers of state under his arm. And it invites the viewer to hold the stare, and engage with the picture: the moment of someone in total control, the catastrophic consequences for others. In the Tudor period the papers might be death warrants, in this particular case perhaps they detail the tragic unfolding of a suicide at the heart of a scandal of state.

Simon Smith
London

Thank you for my autumn copy of *Poetry Review*. I fail to see, however, what Alastair Campbell is doing on the cover. I am not aware that he is a poet, or has any particular link with or interest in poetry – unless, of course, there are those who consider "spin" a poetic form. Nor do I find this photographic portrait in the least bit decorative, with its cold "keep-out-of-my-way" look in the eyes, and the scowling mouth tight-lipped and down at the corners. I should be very grateful if you would enlighten me.

Wanda Barford
London

Thanks for the recent *Poetry Review*, with the photo of Britain's greatest living poet on the front cover . . . the man who, as Heaney would have it, "governs our tongues" . . .

Thomas Docherty
Kent

Jeremy Hooker

I have recently read Andrew Duncan's review of Jeremy Hooker's *Adamah* in *Poetry Review* (93.2). I know *Adamah* well myself, having reviewed the collection for *Planet* (159, June/July 2003).

My judgement of *Adamah* differs from Andrew Duncan's. But that is not the main critical issue. What disturbs me is that *Poetry Review* – which, of all current reviews, should reliably represent and interpret what is happening in British poetry – thought it proper to publish a review which gives the reader so inadequate a notion of the range of work *Adamah* contains, so little insight into the collection's

themes, tones and approaches, and no sense at all of how *Adamah* relates to Jeremy Hooker's previous collections or, indeed, to his recent *Welsh Journal*, rich in related (and, I believe, importantly new) themes. Although Duncan does refer admiringly to *Poetry of Place* and *The Presence of the Past* as "two indispensable works", he fails to relate their critical insights with any subtlety to the considerable body of Hooker's own poetry or to *Adamah* in particular.

Duncan claims at the start to "sign up ... in toto" to "the importance ... of the transcendent" but later insists that "the best modern poetry is driven by Marxism, sexual awakening, and other radical toxins". There seems to be some confusion here. What line are we being asked to toe, personally, critically, above all poetically? In any case, it is, I believe, critically irresponsible to turn phases or strands of the past into prescriptions for viable present or future "making". Cultural, like biological, evolution works on quite other principles, being sensitive to ever-changing contexts and exploratory within them.

So the evaluative question requires attention after all. "What we find missing in Hooker is alienation", proclaims Duncan. But who are "we?" What I value most in Hooker's poetry is precisely its exploratory nature, its honesty, its sense of human existence inhabiting "pasture at the brink of the sea" yet (or perhaps for that very reason) sometimes its ability to see beyond what looks to be the case: ". . . everywhere, fragments of web shining, that look like ends."

To these qualities Duncan seems, at least on the evidence of this review, intellectually and emotionally blind.

Anne Cluysenaar
Gwent

Writing

In Toby Litt's essay on "Writing" in the autumn 2003 issue of the *Poetry Review*, the issues regarding inspiration are very intelligently discussed, but no real conclusions are reached.

The idea of "inspiration", however discredited it may be, survives because it does, to some extent, correspond to the writer's experience, as Toby Litt points out. This is not to say that the finished poem simply jumps onto the page out of nowhere; that would be absurd. No one denies that writing is essentially re-writing, as the experience of all writers everywhere attests. It was undoubtedly true even of oral texts, which were elaborated and reworked over long periods of time before they were written down. But it is also true that technique is not enough. Poe's technique of composition by itself cannot create a poem. Probably no technique can. The starting-point of a poem, story, or novel, or play, is an idea, or image, which may be very vague and ill-defined, but which nevertheless serves as a point of departure. It will become clarified as the writing proceeds, as the writer gradually understands what he wants to do with the idea. The re-writing and clarification is a conscious process, but the mystery is where the starting idea comes from. Sometimes an idea or image seems to appear out of nowhere and to grab one with the force of an obsession. Obviously it is an intuition. It is so important in the writing process that it was given a divine or mythological origin. In modern terms, the source of the intuition may be the unconscious, or even Jung's collective unconscious. What seems to be true in my own experience is that writing which is merely conscious is dry and ineffective, but totally unconscious writing does not exist. The best combination is a mixture of ideas and images coming from the unconscious, and a conscious ordering and elaboration of them.

Certainly a writer must be willing to revise, rewrite and, if necessary, to destroy inferior work. In the case of a poem, it is necessary to know when something in a poem can be saved (maybe only two lines out of one hundred), and when nothing can be saved. Sometimes poems may require only minor revisions.

Gerald Parks
Trieste

The *Poetry Review* Crossword No. 2

The sender of the first correct solution opened on 1 March will receive a cash prize of £20. Entries should be addressed to *Poetry Review* Crossword, 22 Betterton Street, London WC2H 9BX.

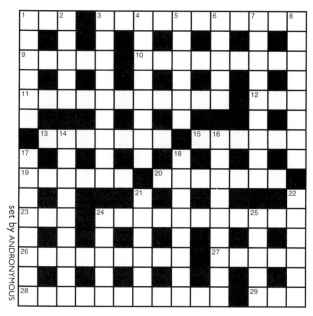

set by ANDRONYMOUS

Across

1 11's incisive text rejecting union (3)
3 Wizard accepts one, not nothing, in return for French fortification (7,4)
9 11's tempestuous spirit (5)
10 Moors are shaken after husky cry from 11's poem (9)
11 Writer is sly, in a way; the Roman way, in the way Latin is (6,5)
12 You're asked to spend a penny on this burning man (3)
13 From 11's novel kind of canto – many sound discordant. (4,3)
15 Soldiers take Spenser's princess to steamy places (6)
19 Capture a woman, and old partner comes back (6)
20 Plans for tiny mints go awry (7)
23 Eggs burst, poisoning several hearts (3)
24 11's work is trivial; came undone (1,2,8)
26 Half a Ricard after Chivas Regal outrages Arthurian (9)
27 11's Pop poem (5)
28 11's big poem – the first schools use for deconstruction (3,8)
29 Dance hit (3)

Down

1 Elegant ship stuck in wet mud (6)
2 Criminal tailor loses nothing in legal process (5)
3 May 1st last month, the Spanish quietly entered into 11, raising a place of many screens (9)
4 Group of Indonesian drums contain phosphorus for match 20 (8)
5 Manufacturer in Japan is sanitised (6)
6 Burn church at foot of hill (5)
7 Carbon-free chemistry rig contains no way to adapt (9)
8 Some of the Sausages say "is there Bacon, perhaps?" (8)
14 Wieners, in state that is in partnership with Morecambe (5,4)
16 It duels at crazy distances overhead (9)
17 Chromium toy car, souped up, conveys baby (8)
18 Sound structures make C ascend through E (8)
21 Wide space – boy r-runs round start of child (6)
22 Misbehave thus, thus, before you play the game (4,2)
24 Final stage of grim agony (5)
25 Oddly, Claude eats a soldier-student (5)

Editorial

There are some arguments in this issue of *Poetry Review*. In his review of Andrew Duncan's *The Failure of Conservatism in Modern British Poetry* – a book he wants to "defend despite its defects and contend with despite its virtues" – Richard Burns takes issue with Duncan's sense of conservatism. Comparing Duncan with the Italian poet Marinetti – a poet who, as Ezra Pound saw it, failed to appreciate the importance of tradition in poetry – Burns contends that, when we are speaking about poetry, "conservatism" has many meanings, many of them positive. These positive meanings are lost sight of, Burns argues, when conservatism is too easily opposed to radicalism. Readers are urged to read *The Failure of Conservatism*, but they are urged also to think beyond it, towards a poetry "embodying generosity, magnamimity, hospitality and inclusiveness".

John Redmond identifies a different kind of newness in his review of Philip Gross's *Mappa Mundi*. "In an age when politicians don't want to sound like politicians (Blair) and businessmen don't want to sound like businessmen (Branson), it shouldn't be too surprising," Redmond thinks, "that poets don't want to sound like poets." What Redmond finds in *Mappa Mundi*, then, a book "with a number of clear strengths", is what he calls "that contemporary tone of voice". But what should a poet sound like? Not one thing, clearly; though for Burns, as for Redmond, whatever they sound like, they should certainly sound as if they have engaged with poetry's past.

What about the artist's own past? How does the individual renew him or herself? In his sparkling and vigorous review of Philip Guston's "Retrospective", Paul Farley wonders, "How many other artists since, or writers for that matter, have managed to wreck and re-invent and make a new space for themselves like this one did?" What Guston wrecked was the "tasteful, painterly abstraction" which had made him so successful. How he re-invented himself was by "lurching … into a big-in-your-face figuration the like of which nobody could have been expecting". Suddenly Guston was painting Richard Nixon, Klansmen, cigarettes, jalopies; what Philip Roth, a friend of Guston's, has called the "crapito" of American life. As Guston himself said, and as Farley quotes approvingly, "I got sick and tired of all that purity. Wanted to tell stories."

And speaking of stories, or rather speaking of "big in-your-face figuration", what on earth was Alistair Campbell doing on the cover of the last issue of *Poetry Review*? "How is this relevant to poetry?", one correspondent asks. How is it not, replies another; Campbell being, as he sardonically puts it, "Britain's greatest living poet … the man who, as Heaney would have it, 'governs our tongues'."

The arguments these contributors are having are substantial. They are about how poetry generates and re-generates itself, and as such are the kind of arguments out of which better poems might emerge.